WILD FLAVOURS
real produce real food real cooking

WILD FLAVOURS

real produce real food real cooking

Mike Robinson

Photography Sebastian Hedgecoe

CASSELL ILLUSTRATED

First published in Great Britain in 2005
by Cassell Illustrated,
a division of Octopus Publishing Group Limited
2–4 Heron Quays, London E14 4JP

This paperback edition pubhished in 2006 by
Cassell lllustrated

ISBN-13: 9781844035168
ISBN-10: 1 84403 516 6

10 9 8 7 6 5 4 3 2 1

Photographs by Sebastian Hedgecoe

Food Styling by Linda Tubby

Design by John Round Design

**Jacket Design and Art Direction
by Auberon Hedgecoe**

Publishing Manager: Anna Cheifetz

Edited by Lesley Malkin and Karen Dolan

Printed and bound in China

Author's acknowledgements
I'd like to dedicate this book to my
wonderful wife Katie, who has been
unbelievably supportive throughout
an extremely busy year.

And great thanks to my lovely agent,
Anne Kibel, whose tireless support and
belief in me has made this book and my
many exciting projects possible.

I would also like to thank a host of
incredibly kind and supportive people:
Gennaro Contaldo for being a great friend
and fount of culinary knowledge, as well
as completely crazy; Joe Wadsack for
being a great friend, and wine supremo;
my parents, Alan and Gilly, for all their
support over the years on my chequered
career path; Tim Reader, my manager at
the Pot Kiln, for his unfailing loyalty and
hard work; and my dog Sassy, for being
the best friend a man could ever have.

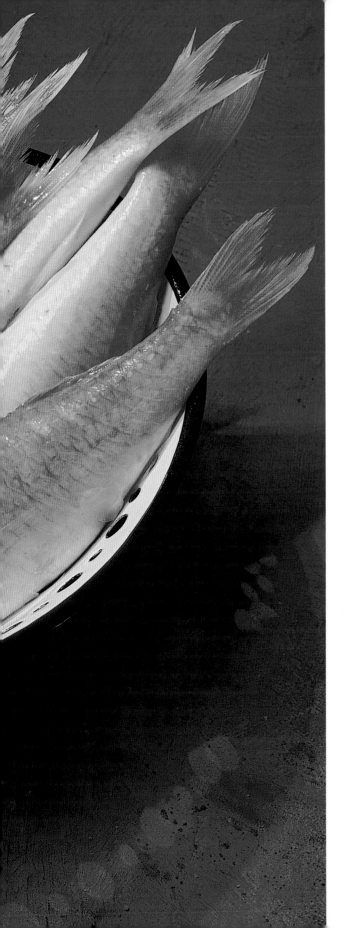

Contents

Introduction

Essentially this book is about 'proper food'. To me, proper food is country food, uncomplicated, simple and delicious. The countryside has always been my life, and that is reflected in my food – good ingredients cooked simply with plenty of flavour. I have included recipes inspired by my experiences in the UK, as well as living and travelling abroad, especially in France, Italy and Spain, which all have outstanding peasant food cultures.

I grew up surrounded by wonderful countryside and as such, of course, surrounded by food. My father loves cooking, and is very, very good at it. His passion for food ignited a spark in me and started me cooking. The gastronomic high points in my childhood were when Dad, who was a long-haul pilot for British Airways, came home. He would always bring goodies from wherever he'd been. Seattle, with its famous Pike Place fish market, was our favourite. I used to love opening the big polystyrene box to reveal fresh Pacific salmon or crab, occasionally some beautiful oysters, wrapped in ice.

At boarding school, along with friends Mike and Ian, I was obsessed with survival and hunting. Using bows and arrows made in woodwork and setting snares, we caught ducks, rabbits and pheasants galore, and learned to prepare them in loads of different ways. About this time I started getting invited to local shoots in the wintertime, and realised that poaching was not really on. My father gave me my uncle's old shotgun, and I was hooked. I asked the gamekeepers for any unsaleable pheasants and partridges, and practised different recipes on them.

One of my tutors at school was a wonderful man called Mr Potts, who was a Master of Wine. I failed his A-level, but did develop an interest in and understanding of wine. When I left school, I worked for a wine merchant, where we had weekly tasting lessons. Luckily for my liver, the shop closed after six months, and I found a job as a forester on a huge private estate in Berkshire. Some of the old foresters had been there for 40 years, and imparted their vast knowledge of the animals, edible mushrooms and plants to me – a real country education.

I decided to study forestry at the University of North Wales, Bangor, where I found a new love: climbing. This led me to the Alps, and Chamonix, which was to be my home for four years. Here I was plunged into the restaurant world, first by economic necessity, and then by love for the work. Very quickly I knew that my future was as a cook. After Chamonix, I knew I wanted to expand my horizons culinarily, but having just spent a few years in the loveliest place in Europe, I couldn't bear the thought of going to gloomy London. So Australia beckoned, and 13 months of intensive, fantastic cooking.

I returned to the UK fired-up, but not wanting to work my usual 15 hours a day in a kitchen – I knew this would be the death knell to a fledgling relationship with my now-wife Katie. Also keen to run my own business, I settled on the idea of a delicatessen. Thinking that a little experience would be a good idea, I cooked for a couple of months in Mr Christian's Deli in Notting Hill (still to my mind the best deli in London) before setting up in Bath.

We stayed for four years until a client offered to buy the place. For some time Katie and I had fantasized about going on a European road trip, so we handed over the keys and set off for three months of driving and eating. We drove through France, eating coq au vin in Burgundy, and fish stew in Provence. We crossed into Spain for seafood paella by a little fishing harbour, then on to Barcelona for a week of tapas.

As if by magic we found ourselves in Chamonix again, just in time for the skiing season. We started a cooking agency called SOS Cuisine, hiring out chefs (me) to wealthy chalet owners on an emergency basis. This worked because the chefs in the chalets were inevitably crazy Aussie snowboarders with a penchant for serious injury.

After two seasons of this, an unknown, just-launched TV channel called UKFood approached me to ask if they could follow me for an episode of a series on posh chalet cooking. I said yes, the filming was done, and a week later they asked if I would present the series. I was dumbfounded, I had no idea what to do or how to talk to a camera, and so naturally I said yes. Thus we made the 'Chalet Slaves' series, which led to 'Good Food Live', first as a guest and then as a presenter. What an experience for a chef! Not only did I learn to present (sort of) with the fabulous Jeni Barnett, but I got to cook regularly with a host of brilliant chefs. Another highlight was a month-long boys'-own culinary adventure around Kenya to make 'Safari Chef': cooking and hunter-gathering in the loveliest place on earth.

Probably the high point in my short TV career, though, and the thing for which I am most grateful to 'Good Food Live', was meeting Gennaro Contaldo, who has become my culinary Godfather. We think in exactly the same way about food, about how it should be seasonal, simple and well-flavoured, and above all we share an abiding passion for the countryside. He has given me endless advice on writing, on recipes, and has rekindled my passion for country food, which I hope is reflected in this book.

Don't be afraid of countryside ingredients. Remember that while you may not find a wild rabbit in your local supermarket, you can get it in a good local butcher. Buying from small shops is very good news, since everyone benefits. You get personal service from knowledgeable people, the produce is not over-packaged and the quality is usually miles better. Shopping is incredibly satisfying when you get to know your local butcher/deli/fishmonger. I realise that the supermarket is inescapable these days, but it is worth going to the little shops whenever you can, particularly for fresh meat and fish.

Every one of the recipes in this book has been a favourite of mine at one time or another, and I hope that if you try them, they will become yours too. One last thing: these recipes need not be followed slavishly. The best sort of cooking is done by feel, and you know what your tastes are: a dash of this, a handful of that, a squeeze or shake of something else: be a little adventurous!

MIKE ROBINSON

soups

introduction

Soup IS country food. Whether it is warming or cooling, hearty or delicate, smooth or chunky, it is always satisfying. For me, soup is always associated with the outdoors. It invariably means winter, with the honourable exception of sitting on the bank of England's River Kennet in June having just landed a good brown trout on a dry fly. This is most definitely a Gazpacho moment, especially if you have had a good bottle of white wine chilling in the mill race all morning.

I have an old vacuum flask made of steel that I must have had for 20 years, that lives with me when I'm outdoors in winter, and it only ever contains soup. Certain pursuits require different soups. Pigeon shooting in a bitterly cold wood in February is always Pea and Ham, whereas rough shooting among the brambles in December is by necessity French Onion. Whatever the time of year, you're sure to find a soup that suits in the following selection.

Chilled red pepper and watercress gazpacho

This is a slight variation on a classic summer gazpacho. Because I am lucky enough to live near several chalk rivers, and do like my fishing, I am always picking handfuls of gorgeous peppery watercress. This fiery watercress adds that certain something that I think gazpacho is often missing. Make sure you serve it really cold, with little bowls of chopped cucumber and pepper, and maybe a chopped red chilli if you are feeling adventurous.

Serves 4

Preparation: 20 minutes, plus 4 hours' chilling

Soup:

250 g/8 oz ripe tomatoes, skinned and chopped

2 onions, chopped

2 large red peppers, deseeded and chopped

½ small cucumber, peeled, halved lengthwise, seeds removed, and chopped

1 small garlic clove, chopped

75 g/3 oz white bread, crusts removed

1 lemon, deseeded and chopped

4 tbsp olive oil

100 ml/3½ fl oz water

splash of sherry vinegar

salt and pepper

Watercress purée:

100 g/3½ oz watercress

50 ml/2 fl oz Chicken Stock (see page 187)

juice of ½ lemon

1 tbsp olive oil

salt and pepper

Put all the soup ingredients in a bowl (setting aside some red pepper pieces for garnish) and allow to macerate in the fridge for several hours.

Meanwhile, make the watercress purée. Blanch the watercress in boiling salted water for 20 seconds, then plunge it into cold water to refresh. Drain, place in a blender or food processor then add the cold chicken stock, the juice of half a lemon and a good glug of olive oil. Blend until smooth then season.

Add a few ice cubes to the gazpacho and process gently in a blender or food processor, leaving some texture in the soup. Spoon into a large serving bowl or individual bowls, swirl the watercress purée around, and decorate with chopped red pepper.

French onion soup

If chicken soup is Jewish penicillin (see opposite), then surely this is the French 'cure-all'. Onion soup must be dark, rich and a bit oily, and requires courage to cook. Courage, you say? Yes, because you have to stand by and deliberately allow the onions to caramelise to the point of burning to get the most out of them. According to the food police, onions and garlic are incredibly good for you, dispersing free radicals (I thought we had got rid of them at the end of the 19th century!) and reducing the risk of heart disease. Well, here you have a wonderfully full-flavoured soup that charges through the body doing you good, and is also just about the cheapest thing you can make.

Serves 6
Preparation: 15 minutes
Cooking: 45–60 minutes

50 g/2 oz butter

10 onions, sliced

3 garlic cloves, crushed

1 tbsp tomato purée

50 g/2 oz plain flour

50 ml/2 fl oz white wine

1.5 litres/2½ pints Chicken Stock (see page 187)

salt and pepper

dash of Cognac (optional)

4 slices French bread, toasted

100 g/3½ oz Gruyère cheese, grated

Start by melting the butter in a really good heavy-based pan over a medium heat. When it foams, add all the onions and garlic and leave them to cook. After 5 minutes or so the bottom onions will start to catch, or almost burn. Now stir them around, and repeat the process until all the onions are seriously dark brown.

Add the purée, and stir in well, then do the same with the flour. Cook for 2 minutes, then add the wine and stock. Bubble away for 40 minutes, until the soup has reduced by a quarter. Season to taste, add a dash of Cognac if you wish, then ladle into deep bowls.

Float a slice of toasted bread on the soup and cover the bread and soup with loads of grated Gruyère. Place under the grill for 3 minutes to melt and bubble. Serve at once with chilled white Burgundy or cider.

Jewish penicillin (chicken soup)

I will probably get in trouble for the title of this recipe, but I had to put it in. This soup is a bit like French Onion Soup in that it supposedly has curative properties. Whenever one of us has a cold, this recipe is prepared and while never exactly the same twice, it always serves its purpose.

Serves 6
Preparation: 30 minutes
Cooking: 2½ hours

1 small whole chicken (approx 1.25 kg/2½ lb)

2 litres/3½ pints water

1 onion, peeled and chopped

2 celery sticks, chopped

1 carrot, chopped

2 tbsp olive oil

3 garlic cloves, chopped

2 potatoes, diced small

2 tbsp pearl barley

1 bouquet garni (thyme, parsley, sage – all renowned for their healing properties)

In a big pan, cover the chicken with the water and bring to the boil. Simmer for 1½ hours, then take out the chicken and let it rest. It should be nearly falling apart in your hands. Now simmer the stock in the pan for 30 minutes, so it reduces by a third.

In another pan, sweat off the onion, celery and carrot in a little olive oil, and add the garlic. Add the vegetables to the stock, along with the potatoes, pearl barley and bouquet garni. Simmer the soup for 30 to 40 minutes. Shred the now cooled chicken with your hands, adding any resulting juices to the soup. Just before serving, discard the boquet garni and stir in half of the shredded chicken. I like to use the thigh meat for the soup and save the breasts for sandwiches or Caesar salads. Sit in front of a fire and a good movie and feel your mood improve.

Peasant's soup

This is perfect country soup, using fresh, simple ingredients and a good hearty stock. I always use chicken stock in this, because I think it makes for a more robust result. If you want to make it veggie, just use really good vegetable stock. You can use canned beans instead of fresh or dried, but add them for only 15 minutes so that they don't overcook.

Serves 6
Preparation: 20 minutes
Cooking: 45 minutes

2 carrots

2 celery sticks

1 large onion, peeled

2 potatoes, peeled

4 tbsp good quality olive oil

3 garlic cloves, crushed, but not skinned or chopped

1 bouquet garni (thyme, parley, sage)

2 litres/3½ pints Chicken Stock (see page 187)

200 g/7 oz fresh borlotti beans or 100 g/3½ oz dried
(make sure you soak the dried beans for 24 hours first, changing the water twice in the process)

salt and pepper

handful of flat-leaf parsley

a small handful of celery heads (the leafy bits at the top)

grated Gruyère or Parmesan cheese, to serve (optional)

Cut the carrots, celery and onion into smallish dice. Do the same with the potato. Glug a hearty amount of olive oil into a heavy pan and let it heat up. Sweat off the veggies, garlic and the potato for a few minutes, just to colour them slightly. Add the bouquet garni and pour in all that glorious chicken stock and bring to a simmer. Now, put in the beans and plenty of salt and pepper.

Simmer for about 30 minutes, or until the beans are just tender, then stir in another glug of oil and the chopped parsley and celery heads. Discard the bouquet garni.

For real winter comfort, liberally dollop grated Gruyère or Parmesan over the soup as it comes to table. Serve really good bread with this – something chewy with a good crust that can take being slathered in butter and dunked in the bowl.

Pea and ham soup

When I lived high in the Alps, my butcher Philippe thought it was really very funny having an English chef living in the village, the words 'English' and 'Chef' being something of an oxymoron to the French. Philippe used to treat me as his personal project, forever giving me strange cuts of meat and offal, together with esoteric cooking instructions and much Gallic hand-waving – I think he was determined to chase all British influence from my cooking. Philippe's low point came when I requested a ham bone one day. 'Pour le chien?' he enquired. I explained I wanted it for an old-fashioned British soup with peas. The poor chap looked quite horrified, but as requested, sawed the bone in half, so the marrow could seep into the soup during cooking. As I left, I could hear the old ladies in the queue muttering about the absurdities of 'rosbif' cooking. A parting shot came through the door: 'Make sure the poor dog gets the bone afterwards.'

Serves 4
Preparation: 10 minutes
Cooking: 40 minutes

50 g/2 oz butter
2 onions, finely chopped
1 garlic clove, finely chopped
small handful of thyme leaves
750 g/1½ lb frozen peas
1 ham bone, sawn in half
1 litre/1¾ pints Chicken or Vegetable Stock (see pages 187 and 188)
salt and pepper
cream, to serve

Heat the butter in a large saucepan over a medium heat and add the onions, garlic, thyme and peas. Cook for 3–4 minutes, stirring constantly. Now add the bone and the stock and bring to a simmer. Simmer for 30 minutes, remove the bone and whizz the lot in a blender. Season to taste, stir in a dollop of good cream and serve with chunks of crusty white bread.

Mountain guide soup

Probably the most basic and peasanty recipe in this entire book. If you are vegetarian, then substitute water or vegetable stock for the chicken stock, and leave out the pancetta – the soup will not suffer too much. Actually soup in this instance is a bit of a misnomer. This is actually a really hearty coarse vegetable broth, almost a stew, and is a complete meal. As the name implies, this is real mountain fare: filling, cheap, and hearty.

Serves 6
Preparation: 20 minutes
Cooking: 40 minutes

25 g/1 oz butter

3 leeks, roughly chopped

3 medium-sized potatoes (preferably Maris Piper), chopped into chunks

1 large onion, chopped

1 turnip, chopped into chunks

1 swede, chopped into chunks

1 small Savoy cabbage, cut into chunks

2 carrots, cut into chunks

3 garlic cloves, 2 chopped, 1 left whole

150 g/5 oz pancetta, finely cubed

100 ml/3½ fl oz white wine

1 litre/1¾ pints Chicken Stock (see page 187)

salt and freshly ground pepper

1 French stick, sliced into rounds

2 tbsp olive oil

200 g/7 oz Gruyère cheese, grated

Heat the butter in a large casserole dish. Put in the leeks, potatoes, onion, turnip, swede, cabbage and carrots and fry gently, stirring often, for 10 minutes.

Add the chopped garlic and pancetta and fry for 1–2 minutes. Pour in the wine and stock and just enough water to barely cover the vegetables, if needed. Bring to the boil, reduce the heat and simmer for 20 minutes. Using the back of a fork, gently crush the vegetables. Season with salt and freshly ground pepper.

Meanwhile, preheat the oven to 200°C/400°F/Gas Mark 6. Place the bread rounds on a baking sheet, rub with the whole garlic clove and brush with the olive oil. Bake for 5 minutes until golden and crispy. Top the vegetable soup with the baked bread rounds and sprinkle over the grated Gruyère.

Place the soup in the oven and cook until the cheese has melted and is golden brown.

Wild crayfish soup

I remember from my schooldays catching crayfish, like mini lobsters, from the river that ran through the school grounds. The crayfish now found in abundance in most rivers in the southern half of England are the American Signal Crayfish, an introduced breed that are bigger and more aggressive, but fortunately for us they are quite delicious, and easy to catch. All you need is a trap, a licence from the Environment Agency and permission to do so.

Serves 6

**Preparation: 1 hour
(mainly peeling crayfish)**

Cooking: 1 hour

Soup:

1 kg/2 lb crayfish, in their shells

1.5 litres/2½ pints Fish Stock
(see page 188)

1 onion, finely chopped

1 celery stick, finely chopped

1 carrot, finely chopped

1 garlic clove, crushed

a splash of white wine

zest and juice of 1 lemon

a pinch of saffron

20 ripe cherry tomatoes

1 red pepper, deseeded and finely diced

1 small red chilli, deseeded and chopped

a splash of Cognac

salt and pepper

2 tbsp olive oil

Rouille:

2 tbsp mayonnaise

zest and juice of ½ lemon,

1 red chilli, deseeded and finely chopped

1 garlic clove, finely chopped

1 pinch cayenne pepper

Croûtons:

4 slices French bread

1 garlic clove

2 tbsp olive oil

Lightly boil the crayfish for 10 minutes in a large saucepan. Turn off the heat and remove the crayfish, reserving the stock. When cool enough to handle, remove the shells from the crayfish and set aside.

Return the pan of stock to the heat and add the onion, celery, carrot and garlic. Bring to the boil, then add the crayfish shells to the stock. Add a splash of white wine, the lemon zest and juice, saffron, cherry tomatoes, red pepper and chilli, and cook for a good 15 minutes.

Take off the heat and add the peeled crayfish. Now use a powerful hand blender to grind the shells, stock and peeled crayfish to make a rich soup. Pass through a sieve into a pan and, over a medium heat, reduce the soup that is left by a third. Add a splash of Cognac and check the seasoning before adding the olive oil.

Mix all the ingredients together to make the rouille. Make the croûtons by rubbing the French bread with garlic, drizzling the slices with a little olive oil, and toasting.

To serve, pour the soup into bowls, then top each with a crisp bread croûton and a little of the rouille.

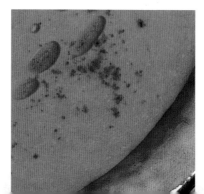

meat

introduction

There is no surer way to inspire a meat-lover to cook than to take them into a traditional butcher's shop, with marble slabs groaning with beautiful cuts of meat and white-clad butchers plying their trade. All the best butchers will have long queues outside on a Saturday, with a line of people anxiously eyeing up the meat they have in mind. Personally, I do not mind the wait, it tells me that people are now really thinking about their ingredients, and are no longer happy to buy anaemic pieces of meat wrapped in clingfilm in their local supermarkets.

For many years I lived in Bath in the west of England, where I had a delicatessen and an outside catering company. Bartlett's, my butcher, was fantastic. The shop has been going for generations, and is exactly what a really good butcher's should be. The beef was always dark and marbled with creamy fat, and had been hung for at least 28 days. The pork had a real rind of fat on it, and obviously didn't come from those skinny torpedo-like pigs that are currently popular. Best of all, though, was the game. Mr Bartlett Senior used to shoot all around the area, and so had the pick of the pheasants, partridges and rabbits to be had locally. Quite often there would be an enormous brown hare hanging just inside the door, or even a roebuck. Oh, and they make the best pork and herb sausages ever.

I learned a lot about meat for myself after my two Gloucester Old Spot pigs ended their outrageously pampered life, yielding a whopping 300 kilograms/600 pounds of meat. With the help of butcher Andy Bartlett, I cured hams, salted and smoked sides of bacon, roasted shoulders of pork to crunchy perfection, and made hundreds of sausages.

That whole episode taught me three things about meat. One: fat is good, it adds flavour and keeps the meat juicy. Two: buy the best quality meat you can afford from a reputable source. Three: always buy your meat from a good local butcher: it will have been properly looked after, hung and prepared (even if they won't give you their recipe for sausages!).

Beef, onion and potato pasty-pie

I think everyone loves a Cornish pasty, with rich chunks of beef, onions and potato, and this recipe is a really straightforward way of making what is, in effect, a giant pasty. I often do this hot for a quick lunch at home, or cold for when I am going out with mates for a day's fishing.

Serves at least 4
Preparation: 20 minutes
Cooking: 30 minutes

500 g/1lb potatoes

300 g/10 oz rump steak, cut into 1 cm/½ in dice or strips

2 onions, peeled and chopped

4 thyme sprigs, leaves removed

1 garlic clove, chopped

200 ml/7 fl oz Beef Stock (see page 184)

1 tbsp tomato ketchup

a splash of red wine

2 x 28 cm/11 in circles of shortcrust pastry (bought pastry is fine)

salt and pepper

2 eggs, beaten

Peel and slice the potatoes and boil them in salted water for 10 minutes until parboiled. Drain and put to one side.

In a hot pan, sear the beef until well-browned, then remove from the pan. Now cook the onions, thyme and garlic until softened and add the beef. Pour in the stock, the tomato ketchup and a splash of red wine and allow most of the moisture to boil away. By now the beef and onions will be ready. The most important thing is not to have the mix too runny.

Preheat the oven to 200°C/400°F/Gas Mark 6. Lay the sliced potatoes on the bottom sheet of pastry leaving a 3.5 cm/1½ in margin around the edge. Season them as you lay them down – you should end up with a layer of potatoes about 2.5 cm/1 in thick. Now spoon the moist beef and onion mix over the top and spread it out. If you have reduced it enough, the juices will not run off the edges. Lay the other sheet of pastry on top and crimp the edges well.

Brush liberally with egg wash and score any pattern you like into the pastry. Cut a tiny hole in the top to allow steam to escape and bake in the preheated oven for 30 minutes.

Seared rib eye of beef with rosti and Madeira

I love this sort of food: it is rich, satisfying and makes brilliant dinner-party fare. It is quite restauranty in style, in that there are several components which are brought together at the last minute, but what works in restaurants also works well for the dinner party. Make as much of the recipe in advance as possible and you will have a stress-free time.

Serves 2
Preparation: 45 minutes
Cooking: 30 minutes

Roast garlic purée:
1 bulb garlic
1 tbsp olive oil, plus extra for rubbing
1 tbsp lemon juice
sprig of thyme
salt and pepper

2 rib eye steaks, about 250–300 g/
8–10 oz each
vegetable oil, for rubbing
black pepper

Rosti:
50 g/2 oz melted butter
1 large baking potato, peeled, grated and squeezed to remove the water
salt and pepper

Sauce:
50 g/2 oz butter
12 small shallots, peeled and left whole
100 g/3½ oz chanterelles (if you can't get these lovely apricot-coloured wild mushrooms, use 25 g/1 oz dried porcinis rehydrated in a little warm water instead)
50 ml/2 fl oz Madeira
50 ml/2 fl oz red wine
50 ml/2 fl oz dark Beef Stock (see page 184)

Make the roast garlic purée first, in advance if you need to. Cut the garlic bulb in half crosswise and rub the cut sides with oil. Roast in the oven at 180°C/350°F/Gas Mark 4 for 30 minutes, then remove. Squeeze out the garlic into a bowl, add the lemon juice, thyme, oil and seasoning, and mix well. Pour into a mini processor and whizz up. Alternatively, pound the mixture in a pestle and mortar.

Preheat a griddle pan until smoking. Rub the steaks with vegetable oil and season with pepper. Add the steaks to the pan for 2 minutes, do not move them around. Turn over, and cook for 2 minutes on the other side. Remove and set aside to rest.

Meanwhile, make the rosti. Add the melted butter to the potatoes, and season. Preheat a pan and place 2 ring moulds in the middle. Spoon in enough potato to make each rosti 1 cm/½ in thick. Remove the moulds and cook for 3 minutes on each side.

While the rosti is cooking, make the sauce. Add half the butter to a pan and heat until it foams. Add the shallots, then a few minutes later, the mushrooms. Pour in the Madeira, red wine and stock, and any juices from the beef pan (to get the juices from the beef pan, pour in a little red wine and deglaze the pan, then pour the contents into the sauce). Reduce for 2 minutes until half the mixture is left. Season and drop in the remaining butter. This will glaze and thicken the sauce.

To serve, place one rosti in the middle of a large plate. Slice each steak into 8 slices and arrange on the rosti. Dot the mushrooms and shallots around the rosti followed by the sauce. Top with the garlic purée.

Steak and chips

Go to any small restaurant in France around lunchtime and you will find steak frites as part of a set menu. The steak will always be blackened on the outside, fairly thin, and running with carmine juices in the middle. It really is the perfect lunch. You should cook the steak 'seignant', or singed: cooking it in a red-hot pan for one minute on each side, then letting it rest for 5 or 6 minutes before serving. The meat will keep cooking for a few seconds after it is taken out of the pan, just enough so it isn't completely raw. This recipe calls for a good-quality pan, capable of being preheated to a really high temperature without buckling.

Serves 2
Preparation: 15 minutes
Cooking: 15 minutes

2 rump steaks, about 175 g/6 oz each

1 tbsp vegetable oil

2 baking potatoes, peeled and cut into chips

sea salt and pepper

1.5 litres/2½ pints duck fat or vegetable oil

a handful of rocket

a handful of watercress

mustard dressing

Preheat either a cast-iron skillet or a griddle pan until smoke shimmers off it. This will take at least 10 minutes on a high heat. Now bash out the steaks to half their original thickness. Rub them with a little oil and season with plenty of pepper. Drop onto the pan, which should explode with smoke, and cook for 1 minute on each side. Remove from the heat and leave to rest for 5 minutes.

Now make the chips. Preheat a deep pan of duck fat or vegetable oil to medium (140°C/275°F), then drop in the potato chips. Cook for 6 or 7 minutes until the chips break easily when bent. The centres should be floury. Remove the chips and drain on kitchen paper. Turn the fat up high, and wait until a chip fizzes insanely when dropped in. Add your chips to the fat and cook again until golden and crisp. Drain and anoint generously with sea salt.

To assemble, toss the salad leaves in dressing and pile on one side of a big oval plate. Lay the blackened steak in the middle and a pile of glorious frites around the side. Serve with Dijon mustard, tomato ketchup and mayonnaise. Oh, and loads of bread and butter.

Beef bourguignon

Just like Coq au Vin, this recipe had to go in, but I include it with great trepidation. It isn't just because it's very '70s but because like the Coq, it is usually ruined. I believe this is because we don't understand the original origins of the dish: it was a way of cooking the cheap and tough cuts of beef. This means we should use unfashionable cuts of beef for this dish: ideally shin of beef and neck. These parts of the animal get a lot of constant use, and so are very fibrous and full of connective tissue. As a result, they are wonderfully gelatinous and flavoursome when slow-cooked. I guarantee that you will never have leftovers when you do this. Done correctly, it is the most utterly moreish and sexy dish I know.

Serves 4 really hungry carnivores
Preparation: 20 minutes
Cooking: 3½ hours

625 g/1¼ lb shin beef, chopped into large chunks

salt and freshly ground black pepper

2 tbsp duck or goose fat (available from your butcher or supermarkets)

50 g/2 oz smoked bacon, diced

4 garlic clove, chopped

18 shallots, peeled and left whole

2 onions, sliced

1 tbsp tomato purée

1 bouquet garni (thyme, rosemary and flat-leaf parsley sprigs)

12 small cep mushrooms, or any mushrooms in season

750 ml/1¼ pints Burgundy wine (or other Pinot Noir)

25 g/1 oz butter

25 g/1 oz flour

Season the shin of beef with salt and freshly ground pepper. Heat half the fat in a casserole dish. Add in the beef and fry until well-browned. Remove the beef, setting it aside, and add the rest of the duck fat to the casserole. Add the bacon, garlic, shallots and onions and fry, stirring now and then, until browned.

Preheat the oven to 165°C/325°F/Gas Mark 3. Mix in the tomato purée and return the beef to the casserole, with the bouquet garni. Add the ceps and pour in enough wine just to cover the beef. Stir well, put a lid on the pan and bring to a simmer.

Transfer the covered casserole dish to the oven and bake for 3 hours until the beef is tender. Using a slotted spoon, lift out the beef and shallots and pile into a serving bowl. Keep warm.

On the hob, bring the sauce up to a simmer. Meanwhile, melt the butter in a separate pan, then add the flour, stirring well to ensure there are no lumps. When combined, whisk the butter mixture into the sauce a little at a time, stirring constantly, until the sauce is thick enough to coat the back of a spoon. Remove the bouquet garni, pour the sauce over the beef and serve with a bowl of buttered new potatoes, some fresh French country bread and a bottle of Burgundy.

Beef fillet with shallots and Guinness

This has become something of a signature dish of mine. It is the ultimate in comfort food, a dish that warms the soul on a dark and gloomy winter's day. The beef should be cut into thick juicy pink slabs, no wafer-thin slices here, please.

Serves 4
Preparation: 20 minutes
Cooking: 30 minutes

2 tbsp olive oil
625 g/1¼ lb beef fillet
12 shallots, peeled
2 red onions, sliced
1 tbsp tomato purée
3 garlic cloves, peeled
600 ml/1 pint Guinness
3 thyme sprigs
salt and freshly ground black pepper
25 g/1 oz butter
1 tbsp flour
mashed potato, to serve
2 tbsp chives, chopped, to garnish

Heat a frying pan until hot. Add in half a tablespoon of olive oil and heat through. Add in the beef and sear on all sides, making sure the fillet is really well-browned all over – you want almost to burn it.

Heat the remaining olive oil in a casserole dish. Add the shallots, red onion, tomato purée and garlic and fry, stirring often, until lightly browned. Add the beef fillet, Guinness and thyme. Season with salt and freshly ground pepper. Bring to the boil, reduce the heat and simmer for 20 minutes. Remove the beef fillet and set aside to rest, keeping warm.

Bring the Guinness mixture to the boil. Meanwhile, rub the butter and flour together until well-mixed. Add this mixture to the sauce a little at a time, stirring it in until absorbed, to thicken the sauce.

Serve the beef with mashed potato garnished with chives, and spoon around the liquor.

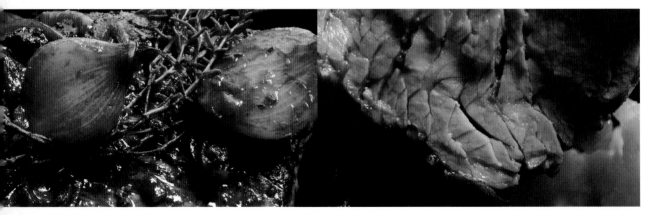

Faggots in Guinness and red-onion gravy

It should be law that every country pub serves this in the wintertime. I know that a lot of people don't like the idea of offal, but once you have tasted this, you will never look back. The flavours are earthy and sublime, and the Guinness gravy is a knockout. I like to serve this with a pan of mustardy mash on the side to soak up the juices. A tankard of real ale is an ideal accompaniment. If you don't have a hand-mincer, use a food processor on the pulse setting, or ask your butcher to mince the beef, kidney and heart.

Serves 4–6

Preparation: 30–40 minutes, plus overnight soaking and resting

Cooking: 50 minutes

50 g/2 oz butter

2 onions, finely chopped

2 garlic cloves, finely chopped

1 tsp chopped parsley

1 tsp chopped sage

1tsp chopped thyme

200 ml/7 fl oz reduced Beef Stock (see page 184)

150 g/5 oz rump steak

150 g/5 oz ox or other kidney

150 g/5 oz ox or other heart

150 g/5 oz chicken livers

salt and pepper

1 egg

50 g/2 oz breadcrumbs

500 g/1lb caul fat, soaked overnight (pre-order this from your butcher)

1 tbsp lard

curly kale, to serve

Guinness gravy:

3 red onions, sliced

1 tbsp lard or dripping.

750 ml/1¼ pints Beef Stock (see page 184)

500 ml/17 fl oz Guinness

sprig of thyme

1 tbsp tomato ketchup

1 tbsp flour

First make the faggots. Melt the butter in a large saucepan and fry the chopped onions, garlic and herbs until translucent, then add the reduced stock and reduce even further, to make a really thick onion juice. Meanwhile, work the beef, kidney and heart through a hand mincer, and chop the livers by hand. Put the meat in a bowl and beat in the salt and pepper, egg, breadcrumbs and finally the onion stock. Rest the mix in the fridge for a few hours.

To make the Guinness gravy, brown the red onion slices in the lard or dripping in a large saucepan until they are soft and coloured, then add the beef stock, Guinness, thyme, ketchup and flour. Reduce the mixture for 30 minutes.

Prepare the faggots while the gravy is reducing. Cut the caul into 12 pieces, and dollop a golf-ball-shaped piece of faggot mix in each. Wrap the caul around the faggot to make a compact ball. Fry the faggots in the lard until they are well-coloured on all sides, and set aside.

Add the faggots to the stock and simmer gently for 10 minutes or so to warm them through. When the Guinness gravy is really thick and rich, the dish is ready. Pile some buttered curly kale in the bottom of each bowl, and sit 2 or 3 faggots on top. Spoon the Guinness and onion gravy around, making sure some onions go on top of the faggots.

Skewered harissa lamb with pepper couscous

Once again, I am venturing a bit south of the Med here, but flavours like these are also much in evidence in the south of Spain and France. This is really impressive stuff when included in your barbecue repertoire, and should seriously impress your neighbours when they lean over the fence to spy on your latest triumph. If you want to really upset them, make the fence higher.

Serves 2
Preparation: 15 minutes, plus marinating
Cooking: 20 minutes

300 g/10 oz leg of lamb, cut into 2.5 cm/1 in cubes

Harissa:
6 red chillies
10 garlic cloves, peeled
small bunch of coriander stalks
zest and juice of 1 lemon
6 tbsp good quality olive oil

Pepper couscous:
200 g/7 oz couscous, cooked
3 peppers, roasted, skinned and finely chopped
zest and juice of 2 lemons
2 tbsp olive oil
small bunch of coriander leaves
salt and pepper

Dipping sauce:
1 tsp harissa
3 tbsp mayonnaise

Whizz up all the harissa ingredients in a food processor until you have a reddish paste. Marinade the lamb cubes in 1 tablespoon of the paste for at least 1 hour. Save the rest in the fridge for use as a killer chilli paste – competitive males will end up experimenting with how much of this they can take on toast.

Skewer the lamb on 8 metal skewers and grill gently over charcoal (remember the coals must be white, not burning) or under a hot grill for 20 minutes.

To make the pepper couscous, mix the cooked couscous with all the other ingredients and season to taste. Divide the couscous between 2 plates, arrange the lamb from 4 skewers on each and mix the harissa and mayo together as a dipping sauce.

Serve with flat bread and cheap tumblers of Moroccan red wine.

Herb-crusted pork fillet with apple and mustard Puy lentils

This recipe came about some weeks after I had dispatched my two beloved Old Spot pigs – Sweet and Sour – to the big piggery in the sky, and was desperately trying to find pork recipes that we were not already bored with. The ingredients happened to be at hand and, as sometimes happens, the recipe actually worked! This is exactly the sort of dish I would choose if I saw it on the menu of a proper country pub.

Serves 2

Preparation: 40 minutes, plus marinating

Cooking: 30 minutes

Marinade:

1 tbsp thyme

1 tbsp rosemary

1 tbsp oregano

2 garlic cloves, chopped

2 tbsp olive oil

1 tsp honey

300 g/10 oz pork fillet (tenderloin)

75 g/3 oz butter

1 red onion, finely chopped

1 eating apple, peeled and finely chopped (I use Granny Smith)

100 g/3½ oz Puy lentils, just-cooked

150 ml/¼ pint cider

1 tbsp wholegrain mustard

1 tbsp honey

salt and pepper

1 tbsp flat-leaf parsley

200 g/7 oz creamy well-seasoned mashed potato

Mix the marinade ingredients together and roll the pork in them. This is such a strongly flavoured marinade that the meat will take on the flavours immediately. Obviously, the longer you leave the pork in the marinade, the stronger the flavour will become. (I recommend about 30 minutes.)

Preheat the oven to 200°C/400°F/Gas Mark 6. Sear the pork in a red-hot roasting pan for 1 minute on each side, then place in the oven for 10 minutes. Remove the pork and rest for at least 5 minutes before carving.

Meanwhile, in another pan, heat 50 g/2 oz of the butter until foaming, add the onion and apple and cook them together for 2 minutes. Now add the lentils and cider, and cook for a few seconds before adding the mustard and honey. Let the lentil mix warm through for 2 or 3 minutes, then season and add the parsley. The idea is to leave enough cidery liquor in the lentils to provide a sauce. At the last minute, stir in the last lump of butter – this will thicken the sauce.

Carve the pork into 1 cm-/½ in-thick chunks. Pile some mash into the middle of a good-sized serving bowl. Lay the pork slices on the mash and spoon the lentils and liquor all around.

Rolled roasted pork belly

Pork belly is the most underrated cut of meat. It is much loved by chefs, who prize it for its flavour and fat content, but it is hard to sell to a public which has been trained to see fat as the ultimate enemy.
I promise you that this dish will convert you. The pork is cooked for long enough that most of the fat is rendered out, leaving juicy, incredibly flavoursome and tender meat encased in the crispiest crackling ever. Also it is unbelievably cheap, and easy to get.

Serves 8
Preparation: 25 minutes
Cooking: 2–3 hours

4 good quality pork sausages
a handful of thyme, chopped
a handful of sage, chopped
2 tbsp wholegrain mustard
2 tbsp honey
2 kg/4 lb piece of boned pork belly
3 garlic cloves, chopped
sea salt and pepper
2 tbsp olive oil

Preheat the oven to 160°C/325°F/Gas Mark 3. Remove the skin from the sausages, and put the meat in a bowl. Add half the chopped thyme and sage, half the mustard, and the honey. Mix well. Rub the meat side of the pork belly with the rest of the herbs, the garlic, and the remaining mustard, and a generous amount of salt and pepper. Squidge the sausage meat down the middle of the belly lengthwise and roll up. Tie the belly up with a piece of cotton string every 2.5 cm/1 in or so. This is painstaking but worthwhile when you come to cut it because it gives you an obvious place to slice through the crackling. Rub the rolled belly with olive oil and salt.

Roast in the preheated oven for 2–3 hours until really golden and crackling. Remove the string, then carve the belly where the string was, into about a dozen thick slices – two slices per person is plenty. I like to deglaze the pan with cider, mustard and cream to make a killer sauce. Serve it with Boulangère Potatoes (see page 142) and Roasted Rosemary Tomatoes (see page 152).

For arguably even better results, you can cook the meat for 8 hours at 110°C/225°F/Gas Mark ¼ , then crisp it up at the end.

Slow-roasted shoulder of pork with braised red cabbage and hasselback potatoes

Don't be put off by the sheer size of a shoulder of pork – it will weigh at least 5 kg/10 lb – this is a dish designed to feed a small army. If that quantity daunts you, ask the butcher for a half shoulder, which will still feed 8 with ease and will cook in two-thirds of the time. Ask for one with plenty of fat under the skin. This will render out during the cooking, keeping the pork really juicy and ensure perfect crackling. The long cooking time makes the meat extremely tender.

Serves at least 12
Preparation: 30 minutes
Cooking: 10 hours (yes, really!)

5–8 kg/10–16 lb shoulder of pork, skin scored

olive oil, for rubbing

2 tbsp chopped thyme

sea salt and freshly ground black pepper

Braised red cabbage:

25 g/1 oz butter

1 red cabbage, cored and chopped

1 onion, chopped

2 Granny Smith apples, peeled and diced

15 ml/½ fl oz malt vinegar

15 ml/½ fl oz Calvados

Hasselback potatoes:

8 large new potatoes or baking potatoes (Maris Piper work well)

50 g/2 oz butter

salt and freshly ground black pepper

2 garlic cloves, finely chopped

25 g/1 oz thyme, finely chopped

75 ml/3 fl oz dry white wine

First of all, let's deal with the pork. A whole shoulder will fit in a domestic oven – just. Preheat the oven to 230°C/450°F/Gas Mark 8 (or as high as it will go). You will need a really big, deep roasting tin. Score the skin of the pork and rub with a little olive oil, fresh thyme and sea salt and sit it on a trivet in the tin. Roast the shoulder for 40 minutes at this heat: the skin will go golden and good things will happen.

Now turn the oven down to 140°C/275°F/Gas Mark 1, and cover the shoulder with a nest of foil. Let it cook for 8 hours (yes, 8 hours), then remove the foil and turn up the heat to 200°C/400°F/Gas Mark 6. Let the pork finish for a further 40 minutes or until you get perfectly explosive crackling. Remove the pork and leave to rest for about 45 minutes, or until the potatoes are done.

Once you have removed the foil from the pork, make the cabbage. Sauté the cabbage, onion and apple for a few minutes in the butter, then add the vinegar. Put the lid on and slow cook for 90 minutes. Just before serving, add the Calvados.

Prepare the potatoes to cook once you've taken the pork out of the oven. Peel them and cut off the bottoms, so they sit on a flat surface. Now run a skewer through the potatoes just above the bottom. Cut down from the top 10 times – the skewer will prevent you going all the way through. Lay all the potatoes in a roasting tin and dot them with butter. Season well, sprinkle with garlic and thyme and pour the white wine around and over them. Roast for 45 minutes or so at 200°C/400°F/Gas Mark 6.

The bones of the pork shoulder should pull out easily, allowing you to pull the meat into pieces. Serve with the braised cabbage, potatoes and proper Gravy (see page 186).

Mountain sausages in white wine
(Diots au vin blanc)

This is basically the French version of sausages with onion gravy. Diots are the wonderful, coarse French mountain sausages. You cannot eat them grilled or fried, but instead have to poach them in a liquid for half an hour or so. If you can't get Diots, buy strong, semi-cured Italian sausages from an Italian deli. We used to eat this dish for lunch in the little mountain 'buvettes' or restaurants in Chamonix, though I suspect you will find the same sort of thing all over the Alps.

Serves 4 (or 2 mountain guides)
Preparation: 10 minutes
Cooking: 40 minutes

2 tbsp duck fat or olive oil

8 Diots, or semi-cured coarse pork sausages

2 onions, finely chopped

2 garlic cloves

2 carrots, diced

2 celery sticks, diced

2 large potatoes, diced small

3 bay leaves

400 ml/14 fl oz white wine

200 ml/7 fl oz Chicken Stock (see page 187)

salt and pepper

buttered cabbage, to serve

This is a one-pan recipe, so I suggest using a big cast iron skillet. Heat the skillet up to hot, and add the duck fat (or olive oil, if you are being healthy). Fry the sausages until they are a good colour all over, then remove them. Add all the vegetables to the pan, and cook until they are soft and have good colour. Now put the sausages back in, and add the bay leaves and white wine. Cook the wine for 5 minutes until it has reduced a little, then add the stock. Simmer until the potatoes are soft, about 20 minutes. Give it 10 more minutes for luck, then season to taste. Serve in a bowl with some buttered cabbage.

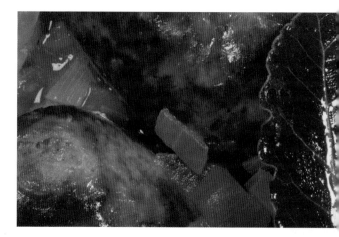

Pork tenderloin with black pudding and a rhubarb and apple sauce

Pork and black pudding – what a combination! When coming up with recipes, chefs tend to err on the side of excess, they always want to add one more ingredient. Well, not in this case, buster: this is one dish that revels in minimalism. So don't add a thing or I will find you and kidnap your hamster.

Serves 2
Preparation: 10 minutes
Cooking: 15 minutes

1 garlic clove, peeled

2 thyme sprigs

1 tbsp olive oil

250 g/8 oz pork tenderloin

200 g/7 oz black pudding

1 Bramley apple, peeled and chopped

2 large sticks rhubarb, peeled and chopped

$\frac{1}{2}$ tsp cinnamon

2 tsp sugar

Preheat the oven to 200°C/400°F/Gas Mark 6. Bash the garlic and thyme together with the oil, and rub over the tenderloin. Sear the loin in a hot pan, then transfer to the oven for 8 minutes.

Meanwhile, cut the pudding into 1 cm/½ in slices and fry in a little oil until crisp on both sides. Cook the apple, rhubarb and cinnamon in a pan with the sugar and a little water for 15 minutes, until broken down.

Lay the slices of pudding on a serving plate, overlapping each other, then slice the tenderloin at an angle into thick slabs. Lay these on top of the black pudding and spoon the sauce around.

Smoked ham hocks slow-cooked with sage, cider and apples

Ham hocks are another cut of meat, like pork belly, that do not get the good press they deserve. These are the piggy equivalent of the lamb shank, and have amazing flavour and texture. They are also incredibly cheap, since nobody seems to want them, as they are seen as fatty and tough. The answer to this, as with pork belly, is to cook them long and slow. This renders out the fat, and breaks down the fibres. Cooking them with cider is excellent, as the sharp apple flavours counteract any remaining tendency to oiliness. One ham hock will do two people happily.

Serves 4

Preparation: 30 minutes, plus 12 hours' soaking

Cooking: 2½ hours

2 large smoked ham hocks

1 tbsp vegetable oil

4 Granny Smith apples, cored and cut into 6

2 large red onions, sliced

1 garlic clove, squashed

2 tspb of wholegrain mustard

1 tbsp honey

600 ml/1 pint strong cider

100 ml/3½ fl oz double cream

small bunch of sage

sauté potatoes, to serve

Because the hocks are smoked, they are very salty, so before cooking, you must soak them overnight in a sinkful of fresh water. In the morning, drain them, refill the sink and soak for 2 more hours. Make sure you dry them well before cooking. You will need a heavy casserole for this dish.

Preheat the oven to 160°C/325°F/Gas Mark 3. On the hob, heat the casserole and add a splash of vegetable oil. Brown the hocks on all sides until well-coloured then remove them. Add the sliced onions, apples and squashed garlic. After a couple of minutes, add the mustard and honey. Now put the hocks back in, and pour over the cider. Put on the lid and pot roast in the oven for 2½ hours. When the hocks are done, the meat will have shrunk back from the bone and will be falling-apart tender. Remove the hocks and pull the meat off the bone, discarding the skin.

Put the casserole on the hob and add the double cream to the mixture. Let it bubble away for a minute, and add some ripped-up sage leaves. Pile the ham on some sauté potatoes, and ladle the oniony, appley sauce over and around.

Ham pot-au-feu

Although the name is French, this is the sort of thing that can be found in any European country. The name roughly translates to 'pot on the fire' and there are no hard or fast rules about its contents. At its simplest, this is a concoction of cured meat, root vegetables and grains, cooked with water or stock in a heavy pot over an open fire. It is probably one of my favourite recipes of all time. Oh, by the way, a good free-range chicken works just as well.

Serves 4
Preparation: 25 minutes
Cooking: 2 hours 10 minutes

8 Toulouse or other spicy sausages
1 smoked ham hock (approx 1 kg/2 lb)
125 g/4 oz smoked bacon, cut into strips
50 g/2 oz pearl barley
3 carrots, chopped
2 onions, quartered
4 garlic cloves, skin on
4 potatoes, cut into big chunks
2 leeks, coarsely chopped
1 red pepper, cored, deseeded and sliced
1 small Savoy cabbage, quartered, core removed
1 tsp ground turmeric
2 tbsp vegetable bouillon
1 bouquet garni (a bundle of thyme, sage, parsley and rosemary)
salt and freshly ground black pepper

To serve:
croûtons
1 tbsp pesto sauce
flat-leaf parsley, chopped

Preheat the oven to 190°C/375°F/Gas Mark 5. Heat a griddle pan until hot. Place the sausages on the griddle and cook briefly until lightly browned all over.

Place the ham hock in a large casserole dish, then add the bacon, sausages, pearl barley, carrots, onions, garlic, potatoes, leeks, red pepper, cabbage, turmeric, bouillon and bouquet garni. Season with salt and freshly ground pepper. Pour in enough cold water to cover the ingredients, cover the casserole dish and bake in the oven for 2 hours.

To serve, take the ham and sausages out of the pot, and carve the ham into thick slabs. Remove the bouquet garni and crush the vegetables gently with the back of a fork to release their flavours, then ladle the vegetables and broth into each bowl. Lay a couple of slabs of ham and a couple of sausages on top, and sprinkle on some croûtons, a little pesto and parsley to finish. Serve with plenty of good rustic bread and a robust red wine.

Lamb, thyme, and flageolet beans

Make sure you buy eye fillets of lamb for this dish, not neck fillets. Trim off all the excess sinew and fat, so you are left with only the beautiful dark meat. Do make sure your frying or griddle pan is smoking hot before adding the fillets – the idea is to get the lamb magnificently dark and crunchy on the outside, and meltingly pink and tender in the middle. Oh yes, and remember – all you are doing to the beans and tomatoes is warming them through to release their flavours.

Serves 2

Preparation: 20 minutes

Cooking: 15 minutes

1 tbsp finely chopped sage

1 tbsp finely chopped thyme

2–3 garlic cloves, finely chopped

splash of olive oil

2 lamb fillets, weighing about 175 g/6 oz each

generous knob of butter

½ tbsp plain flour

100 ml/3½ fl oz red wine

salt and freshly ground black pepper

Beans:

1 x 400 g/13 oz canned flageolet beans, drained and rinsed

1 red onion, finely chopped

2 garlic cloves, chopped

2 thyme sprigs

125 g/4 oz cherry tomatoes, quartered

1 tbsp chopped flat-leaf parsley

2 tbsp olive oil

splash of balsamic vinegar

good squeeze of lemon juice

salt and freshly ground black pepper

Pound the sage, thyme, garlic and olive oil to a thick paste, using a pestle and mortar. Smear this over the lamb fillets, then set aside.

Put the beans, red onion, garlic, thyme, tomatoes and parsley in a saucepan with the olive oil. Place over a medium heat and simmer for 3–4 minutes, stirring, to heat through. Add a splash of balsamic vinegar and a squeeze of lemon juice. Season with salt and pepper. Set aside and keep warm.

Heat a heavy-based frying pan over a medium-high heat until hot. Add the lamb and sear for 2 minutes on each side. Transfer to a warm plate.

Reduce the heat to medium-low. Add the knob of butter to the pan. Sizzle for a few seconds, scraping up any sediment from the pan. Sprinkle in the flour and stir for 30 seconds. Stir in the wine, bring to the boil, then simmer for a minute or two until thickened and slightly reduced. Season with salt and pepper.

To serve, spoon the bean mixture onto warm serving plates. Slice each fillet on the diagonal into 6 pieces and lay on top of the beans. Drizzle a little good quality olive oil over the lamb and beans, and pour the red wine sauce around.

Lancashire hot pot

My mother's family come from Lancashire, England, near a little village called Parbold, so this recipe has a special place in my culinary heart. I think it typifies everything that is right about one-pot cooking. It takes very little effort, it is delicious, filling and warming, and is very cheap to make. When I was writing this, I thought I'd probably better get the recipe OK'd so I sent it to my Grannie Christine. She said she thought it looked 'about right', so I now feel justified in including it. I think cider is the best drink to accompany this recipe.

Serves 4–6
Preparation: 30 minutes
Cooking: 1½ hours

25 g/1 oz butter
150 g/5 oz diced carrots
150 g/5 oz diced swede
150 g/5 oz celery
3 onions, sliced
1 tbsp dripping or lard
500 g/1 lb neck or chump of lamb or mutton, cut into small cubes
salt and pepper
3 thyme sprigs
500 ml/17 fl oz Lamb Stock (see page 184)
4 large potatoes, peeled and sliced
buttered Savoy cabbage, to serve

Preheat the oven to 160°C/325°F/Gas Mark 3.

First, fry the vegetables (except the potatoes) in the butter for a few minutes until they are softened. Remove from the pan and add the dripping. When the dripping is hot, fry the lamb for about 5 minutes.

Now it is really just an assembly job. Mix the lamb and the vegetables together in a large casserole dish, and season well. Add the thyme sprigs and pour over the stock. Now add the potato in two or three layers over the lamb and vegetables, and press them down into the stock.

Bake in a moderate oven for 90 minutes. The lamb will be tender and falling apart and the potatoes golden and crunchy. Serve in a deep bowl with buttered Savoy cabbage and bread.

Slow-roast spiced leg of mutton with swede mash

Mutton, I am happy to report, is making something of a comeback after decades in the doldrums. This recipe is very old, dating back to the 1700s when the idea of eating a lamb was ridiculous. After all, why eat something that is only a quarter grown? The flavour of mutton is much stronger than lamb, it is texturally more fibrous and there is a good deal more fat. As a result, I think mutton is better cooked long and slow. This allows the fibres to break down and the fat to render out before it is eaten. This is a real flavour-packed treat. A boned shoulder can be used instead of leg.

Serves 6–8
Preparation: 30–40 minutes
Cooking: 3½ hours, plus resting

1 mutton leg joint, about 3kg/6 lb, boned
1 tbsp duck fat or dripping
½ tsp black pepper
½ tsp fresh thyme leaves
½ tsp ground mace
125 g/4 oz of fine oatmeal
1 Savoy cabbage
200 ml/7 fl oz cider

Mash:
2 leeks, chopped
salt and freshly ground black pepper
2 generous knobs of butter
1 medium swede, peeled and diced

Preheat the oven to 160°C/325°F/Gas Mark 3. Rub the joint well with the duck fat or dripping, black pepper, thyme, mace and fine oatmeal – do not use salt. Wrap the whole joint in cabbage leaves, then tie with string. Place in a tin and cover the tin tightly with foil (traditionally the meat would have been thickly covered in mutton fat).

Roast the joint very slowly, allowing 20 minutes per 500 g/1lb of meat – this joint will take about 3–3½ hours. Baste well at least twice during cooking and when basted, add the cider to the fat in the pan. Once cooked, allow the joint to rest for 15 minutes.

Boil the leeks for about 15 minutes until soft. Drain, season with salt and pepper and add a knob of butter. In another pan, boil the swede until cooked through. Combine the leeks and swede and mash. Season with salt and pepper and add another generous knob of butter.

Serve in old-fashioned style. Carve the boned joint into thick steaming slabs and present on a huge serving platter, with the leek and swede mash piled around, and serve the juices separately as gravy. Flagons of ale will complete the meal.

Foil-baked lamb shoulder with peppers and herbs

This is one of my all-time party favourites. Although you can cook it in the oven, I usually dig a hole in the garden and fill it with charcoal. Once the coals are burning well, I bury the shoulder and cover it with earth. You can leave it for up to 4 hours, as it is well protected by foil. The intense heat will colour the meat beautifully, and the lamb will fall apart when you try to cut it. All the juices that have accumulated in the inner foil bag will have left the meat wonderfully juicy, and will make a fantastic gravy.

Serves 6–8

Preparation: 20 minutes

Cooking: 1½ hours

1 bunch each of rosemary, oregano, thyme, marjoram

2 bulbs garlic

splash of olive oil

salt

6 black peppercorns

1 lamb shoulder, about 1.5 kg/3 lb, boned but with the knuckle left in

2 red peppers, cored, deseeded and sliced

500 g/1 lb new potatoes

500 g/1 lb carrots, roughly chopped

500 g/1 lb parsnips, roughly chopped

glug of olive oil

2 lemons, sliced

30 g/1 oz flour

30 g/1 oz butter

red wine for the gravy, to taste

sea salt and pepper

Preheat the oven to 220°C/425°F/Gas Mark 7. Keeping aside a small amount of the herbs for the vegetables, pound the rest of the herbs, 1 bulb of garlic and a few drops of olive oil in a mortar until you have a coarse paste, then add salt and the peppercorns.

Lay the lamb skin-side down. Slash the meat deeply with a sharp knife. Rub the herb paste into the cuts then lay the peppers on top. Roll the lamb up and tie with two or three pieces of cotton string (you don't have to do this). Rub any remaining paste on the outside. Roll into 3 or 4 layers of foil and bake for 1½ hours.

Next prepare the vegetables. Lay a big sheet of foil down and place the new potatoes, carrots, parsnips, the remaining garlic, olive oil, lemon slices and reserved herbs on it. Season well and seal. After the lamb has been cooking for 30 minutes, put the vegetables in the oven and bake for 1 hour.

Remove the lamb from the oven and allow to rest for 15 minutes. Keep the vegetables hot. To make the gravy, mix the foil bag juices from the lamb with the flour and butter, add a little red wine, then whisk over a medium heat until thickened. Slice the lamb and serve surrounded by the vegetables. Serve the gravy separately.

Leg of lamb with anchovies and a rosemary, marjoram and garlic crust

Serves 8

Preparation: 20 minutes,
plus 20 minutes' resting

Cooking: 1¼ hours

2.75 kg/5½ lb leg of lamb, French-trimmed (knuckle-end trimmed so that the bone sticks out) and with the H-bone removed

100 g/3½ oz jar of anchovy fillets in oil, drained

a bunch of rosemary

a bunch of marjoram

4 garlic cloves, chopped

sea salt

6 black peppercorns

splash of olive oil

Preheat the oven to 200°C/400°F/Gas Mark 6. Make small incisions all over the lamb, and fill them with the anchovy fillets.

Strip the leaves off the rosemary and, using a sharp knife to make a cavity, insert the stalks up the length of the leg bone. Finely chop the rosemary leaves and marjoram. Using a pestle and mortar, pound together the rosemary, marjoram, garlic, sea salt, peppercorns and enough olive oil to make a thick paste.

Smear the rosemary paste all over the leg, place it on a rack in a roasting tin and place in the oven. After 30 minutes, reduce the heat to 180°C/350°F/Gas Mark 4 and cook for a further 45 minutes for a medium-rare roast. (Allow another 20 minutes for medium and another 20 minutes on top of that for well-done.

Remove the lamb from the oven, cover with foil and rest for 20 minutes.

Slow-braised veal shanks with polenta

I love really well-flavoured veal, although I appreciate that veal can be a sensitive issue. If you buy rose veal, i.e. pink-coloured veal, it will have had a good, if short, life, and it is no different from eating lamb. Please do not buy pure white veal – the poor calf will never have seen the light of day. This recipe works a treat. You must use shank for this, as the marrow in the bones seeps out and flavours the braising liquid. The ripe tomatoes break down into the olive oil to give a glorious colour and richness to the dish.

Serves 4

Preparation: 15 minutes

Cooking: 2 hours

4 veal shanks, cut like Osso Bucco, i.e. sawn into 2.5 cm/1 in thick rounds, bone and all

3 tbsp flour, for coating

2 tbsp oil

2 leeks, thickly sliced

4 garlic cloves, sliced

300 g/10 oz vine tomatoes, kept whole

250 ml/8 fl oz white wine

750 ml/1¼ pints Chicken Stock (see page 187)

1 tbsp grated lemon zest

1 tbsp small thyme sprigs

salt and pepper

Polenta:

200 g/7 oz instant polenta

100 g/3½ oz butter

100 ml/3½ fl oz double cream

2 tbsp flat-leaf parsley, chopped

salt and pepper

Preheat the oven to 180°C/350°F/Gas Mark 4. Toss the shank pieces in flour and shake off any excess. Place half of the oil in a large, deep frying pan over a high heat. Add the meat and cook until well-browned. Line the bottom of a large baking dish with the meat. If the meat is in layers, be sure to move them around during cooking to immerse them all in liquid.

Add the remaining oil to the pan and cook the leeks and garlic until golden. Transfer to the baking dish with the tomatoes, wine, stock, lemon zest, thyme, salt and pepper. Cover the dish tightly and bake for 1 hour 45 minutes.

Cook the polenta as instructed on the packet. At the end, mix in the butter and cream and allow it to melt and loosen the polenta, making a creamy bed on which to serve the veal. Add the parsley and season liberally – polenta can taste bland otherwise. Drizzle the sauce from the baking dish on top.

fish

introduction

I have always been obsessed with the idea of catching my own ingredients, and none more so than fish. I first went fishing aged about eight; my first rod consisted of a piece of hazel, some line, a hook and a worm and it worked a treat. I must have caught and kept twenty of those little fish, only to find out on my return home that they were inedible and the lakes were supposed to be catch-and-release.

I suppose my real introduction to the brilliance of fish and seafood was as a young chef in Australia. Here was a sunny land of outdoor cafés, simple Asian-style menus, and happy smiling people. I ended up in Port Douglas, near Cairns, working in a restaurant on the marina. The marina was full of fishing boats, one belonging to Oskar, the restaurant owner. Every day the boat would go out to fish on the reef and whatever the skipper and deckhand caught would come to the restaurant that evening, often still flapping. It was a real education to have 11 kinds of fish arrive at 5pm every day, then to devise a menu, prepare the fish and be ready by 7pm! We cooked everything, from 1.8m/6-foot long Spanish mackerel, to gleaming red emperor snappers, to menacing brown mud crabs. What that job taught me, however, has stuck forever — the importance of cooking fish that is really fresh.

Since returning to the UK, I have fallen in love with the art of fly fishing. My family has to put up with endless recipes for trout and salmon, the result of many happy hours spent on a riverbank in some of the most beautiful countryside in Britain, pursuing this most esoteric of sports.

As with so many things in life, I think the key to cooking fish well is simplicity: don't muck around with it too much and, for goodness' sake, don't overcook it.

Arbroath smokie pâté with instant oatcakes

These little devils are just about the best smoked fish out there. All you need to do is pull the skin off and flake the smoked meat away from the bone with your fingers. Buy more than you need, since these guys are highly moreish, and you will eat a lot while you are whipping up this little number. If you can't get smokies, use smoked haddock that you have grilled and allowed to cool.

Serves 4 as a starter
Preparation: 10 minutes
Cooking: 10 minutes

Pâté:

2 Arbroath smokies (or 2 x 250 g/8 oz smoked haddock, grilled)

2 tbsp butter

1 leek, finely chopped

juice of 1 lemon

200 g/7 oz mascarpone cheese

100 ml/3½ fl oz double cream

small bunch of dill, finely chopped

4 spring onions, finely chopped

Oatcakes:

100 g/3½ oz fine oatmeal

200 g/7 oz plain flour

1 egg

2 tsp baking powder

water, to moisten

salt

To make the pâté, take the flesh off the smokies, and mash in a bowl with a fork. Melt the butter in a small frying pan, add the leek and gently cook until softened. Stir this into the smokies, add all the other pâté ingredients and mix well.

To make the oatcakes, mix the ingredients together and add enough water to allow the mixture to form a firm dough. Take small pieces of the dough and flatten them into circles with a thickness of 1 cm/½ in.

Dry-fry the oatcakes in a medium-hot, heavy pan for 3 minutes on each side, until they have risen slightly. Alternatively, preheat the oven to 200°C/400°F/Gas Mark 6 and bake them for 10 minutes. Serve them warm with butter and the smokie pâté.

Grilled cod with a saffron and shellfish broth

Without doubt my favourite place for seafood is the French Mediterranean coast. This is a very simple recipe, oozing with Mediterranean flavours. The thick, juicy cod works beautifully with the bouillabaise-like broth. I like to eat the cod straight off, then work on the broth with chunks of bread dipped in the rouille. To be more authentic, use red mullet or gurnard instead of cod.

Serves 2
Preparation: 20 minutes
Cooking: 15 minutes

2 cod fillets, 3 cm/⅛ in thick
2 tbsp olive oil
salt and freshly ground pepper
1 carrot, finely chopped
1 celery stick, finely chopped
1 medium onion, finely chopped
1 fennel bulb, finely sliced
1 garlic clove, peeled and chopped
10 very ripe cherry tomatoes, halved
150 ml/¼ pint Fish Stock (see page 188)
100 ml/3½ fl oz white wine
pinch of saffron strands
12 small raw clams
12 raw mussels

Rouille:
4 tbsp mayonnaise (home-made is best)
pinch of cayenne pepper
pinch of ground cumin
2 garlic cloves, finely chopped
1 red chilli, deseeded and finely chopped
zest and juice of 1 lemon
1 tsp ketchup

Preheat the grill to medium-hot. Rub the skin of the cod with a little of the olive oil and season liberally with salt and freshly ground pepper. Place the cod low down under the grill and cook for 12–15 minutes without turning.

Meanwhile, in a heavy-based frying pan sweat the carrot, celery, onion and fennel in the remaining olive oil over a low heat for 5 minutes until softened, stirring often.

Add the garlic and tomatoes, mixing well. Pour in the fish stock and white wine and bring to the boil. Add in the saffron, clams and mussels. Cook for 3 minutes, then remove from the heat.

Meanwhile, make the rouille. In a bowl, mix the mayonnaise with the cayenne, cumin, garlic, chilli, lemon zest and juice and ketchup. Place the grilled cod in a deep bowl, spoon the shellfish broth around the fish and spoon over some rouille. Serve at once.

Risotto of wild freshwater crayfish

I love risotto and had to have one in this book. The right rice is vital. All of the three types of risotto rice available – arborio, carnaroli, and vialone nano – work well. I like carnaroli, mainly because I like the name. You can substitute prawns for crayfish in this recipe, but if you can get crays in season, do use them. As well as being cheap and plentiful, they are hugely underrated as an ingredient, being easily the equal of tiger prawns. Try to buy them live, as then you can extract the maximum flavour. Since they come in all sizes, from tiddly to quite large, I like to use the small ones for stock, and the large for tail and claw meat.

Serves 4

Preparation: 25 minutes

Cooking: 20 minutes

24 large crayfish, peeled and jointed (keep 2 unpeeled aside for garnish), or 200 g/7 oz tiger prawns

2 tbsp olive oil

25 g/1 oz butter

1 large onion, finely diced

1 clove of garlic, crushed

1/4 mild chilli, deseeded and finely chopped

1/2 fennel bulb, finely chopped

300 g/10 oz carnaroli rice

1/2 glass of white wine

1–1.5 litres/1³/₄–2¹/₂ pints of Shellfish Stock (see page 188)

pinch of saffron

small bunch of flat-leaf parsley, chopped

squeeze of lemon (optional)

salt and pepper

Use a large, heavy-bottomed pan to make the risotto. Heat the oil and half the butter, add the onion, garlic, chilli and fennel and sweat over a medium heat. Once the vegetables are soft, add the rice and stir gently for 2–3 minutes. By now all the rice will be coated with oil and the starch will start coming out. Add the wine to the pan and stir for 2 minutes. Now you can add some of the hot stock. A couple of ladlefuls will do for the time being. Add the saffron strands, then some more stock.

Remember, this is an inexact science, and you can only add stock a little at a time. Taste the rice constantly, until it has just a little bite left and the risotto is gloopy but not runny. Now stir in the crayfish tails and claws if they are big enough (or prawns), a little chopped parsley and possibly a squeeze of lemon. Check for seasoning and serve decorated with whole crayfish.

Shellfish lemon sole, Gallic-style

I have always felt that a sole on its own is not quite filling enough, so I added some shellfish, pastis and cream just to make things a bit richer. The flavours all complement the delicate flavours of the sole and do not overpower each other. Pastis, of course, is perfect with shellfish, and the lemon cuts the cream nicely. It is impossible to make this look really neat on a plate, so I don't bother.

Serves 2

Preparation: 15 minutes

Cooking: 10 minutes

65 g/2½ oz butter

2 lemon sole, about 500 g/1 lb, slashed deeply 3 times on each side

4 garlic cloves, finely chopped

juice of 1 lemon

sea salt and freshly ground black pepper

2 shallots, finely chopped

½ fennel bulb, finely chopped

6 raw clams

6 raw mussels

6 raw cockles

250 ml/8 fl oz white wine

100 ml/3½ fl oz pastis

2 tbsp double cream

large handful of finely chopped parsley

In a large ovenproof frying pan, heat half of the butter until it foams. Meanwhile, preheat the grill to high.

Add the lemon sole to the pan and sprinkle the top of the fish with a quarter of the garlic and half the lemon juice. Dot with a little of the remaining butter and season with sea salt and freshly ground pepper. Place the pan under the hot grill and cook the lemon sole for 6–10 minutes, checking often to make sure that the fish does not burn.

Meanwhile, heat the remaining butter in a heavy-based frying pan. Add the shallots, remaining garlic and the fennel and cook for 5 minutes or until softened, stirring often.

Add the clams, mussels, cockles, white wine and the remaining lemon juice to the shallot mixture. Cook over a high heat, stirring, for 2 minutes. Pour in the pastis and double cream and cook over a low heat, stirring, for a further minute until the mixture has reduced and thickened.

Season with salt and freshly ground pepper. Mix in the parsley (reserving a little). Transfer the grilled lemon sole to a serving plate and spoon over the shellfish sauce. Sprinkle over the remaining parsley and serve at once.

Fresh tagliatelle with crab, tomato and garlic

There are very few pasta recipes in this book. I suppose that's because throughout my childhood and early cooking years pasta was always dreadful. I cooked this for the first time in Chamonix in the winter of 2000, and I reckon it's the best pasta recipe ever. I had been called in to cook for a chalet full of very rich Russians and Italians, who rejected the meal I had prepared out of hand. One Italian then came over, and asked charmingly if he could cook, as he had a recipe he wanted to do of his aunt's. What he did was a shining example of simplicity and flavour that really changed my whole outlook on pasta. I have been cooking it ever since. It is essential to use fresh pasta in this recipe.

Serves 4
Preparation: 10 minutes
Cooking: 20 minutes

200 ml/7 fl oz olive oil

4 cloves garlic, squashed and chopped

½ red chilli, left whole

300 g/10 oz ripe cherry tomatoes, halved

300 g/10 oz fresh tagliatelle

250 g/8 oz white crabmeat, or the same amount of tinned white crab

salt and freshly ground black pepper

bunch of flat-leaf parsley, chopped

good squeeze of lemon juice

Pour all the oil into a wide, heavy saucepan. It should be about 3–5 mm (⅛ – ¼in deep). I know this sounds like a lot, but trust me, it works. Heat the oil to medium, not hot, since this recipe is all about gentleness and delicacy. Now add the garlic and the chilli. Allow the garlic and chilli to infuse for 3 minutes or so, then discard the chilli.

Keep the pan on the same heat and add the tomatoes. Let them simmer for 10 minutes, until they start to go squishy. The oil will have taken on a beautiful golden-orange hue at this point.

Plunge the pasta into a big pan of boiling salted water for 3 minutes, then drain thoroughly. Now add the crab to the tomato and oil and stir gently, just to warm it through. Season the mixture, then add the pasta to the pan. Stir off the heat for a moment or two. You will see the oil soaking into the fresh tagliatelle.

Season, add a good squeeze of lemon and a scattering of parsley and divide between bowls. Finish with the tomatoes from the bottom of the pan and a little more parsley.

Frøya scallops with beurre blanc

I recently discovered these scallops – the biggest I have ever seen – from the coast of Norway. What's great about them is that due to the rocky sea bottom they cannot be dredged, which is a horribly destructive and unecologically friendly way of fishing. If you cannot get Frøya scallops, local scallops are wonderful too, but look for diver-caught ones and always buy them in the shell and alive. If they are bashed up and chipped around the edges, please don't buy them – it means they were certainly dredged. This recipe is a bit cheffy, but perfect. The beurre blanc does not overpower the delicate nature of the scallops, it complements them.

Serves 4
Preparation: 5 minutes
Cooking: 15 minutes

1 bulb of fennel, sliced

300 g/10 oz butter, chilled and diced into small pieces

juice of 1 lemon

½ glass white wine

2 shallots, finely chopped

12 Frøya or other scallops

1 tbsp chopped parsley or fennel tops

salt and pepper

First sauté the fennel over a medium heat in a little of the butter. You don't want it to colour, just to soften. After 5 minutes or so, add a squeeze of lemon and a splash of the wine. Allow the liquid to gently cook away, then set the fennel aside.

Now make the beurre blanc. Sweat the shallot in a little butter until it becomes translucent. Add the rest of the wine and most of the lemon juice and allow the liquid to cook away until there is about a tablespoon left. Now, over a low heat, start adding the remaining butter a couple of pieces at a time, saving a knob to cook the scallops in. It is best to use a small whisk to do this. The sauce will emulsify, gradually building up to a rich velvety mixture once all the butter is in. Season the sauce and pass it through a sieve to get rid of the bits. Turn off the heat and keep the sauce warm, giving it an occasional whisk to stop it from separating.

Finally, cook the scallops. Leave the gorgeous red coral on the scallops – for me this is the best bit and adds colour to the dish. Heat a pan to very hot and throw in a knob of butter. Immediately add the scallops and cook for 90 seconds on each side. Just before you take them out of the pan add a squeeze of lemon juice.

To serve, pile the fennel in the middle of the plate and sit 3 scallops on top. Spoon the beurre blanc around and sprinkle a little parsley over the top.

Fish pie, my way

I have long thought that a really good fish pie takes some beating. This one is quite posh, with French overtones (the fennel adds a real Gallic touch). If you want to really tart it up, add a drop of Pernod or pastis and a handful of mussels. This is best served with a simple green salad on the side and a glass of chilled rosé wine.

Serves 4
Preparation: 25 minutes
Cooking: 25 minutes

Béchamel sauce:
25 g/1 oz butter
2 tbsp plain flour
200 ml/7 fl oz milk
salt and freshly ground black pepper

Mashed potatoes:
5 large potatoes, peeled and cut into large chunks
75 ml/3 fl oz milk
25 g/1 oz butter

Filling:
25 g/1 oz butter
1 onion, chopped
1 leek, chopped
2 celery sticks, chopped
1 bulb fennel, chopped
2 garlic cloves, crushed
50 ml/2 fl oz white wine
2 cod fillets, each 175 g/6 oz
juice of 1 lime
bunch of flat-leaf parsley, chopped
250 g/8 oz prawns, cooked
1 egg, beaten

First make the béchamel sauce. Heat the butter in a saucepan over a moderate heat and stir in the flour. Cook for 1 minute, stirring continuously. Stir in the milk, beating with a balloon whisk until smooth. Season to taste with salt and freshly ground black pepper. Set aside.

Next cook the potatoes for the mash in plenty of boiling, salted water until soft. Drain and mash them. Stir in the milk and butter. Set aside in a warm place.

Preheat the oven to 200°C/400°F/Gas Mark 6. Heat the butter in a frying pan over a moderate heat and fry the onion, leek, celery, fennel and garlic together for about 5 minutes, until softened but not coloured. Add the wine. Chop the fish into bite-sized pieces and add to the pan. Add the béchamel and cook for 3–4 minutes.

Add the lime juice and parsley. Stir in the prawns. Spoon the mixture into an ovenproof dish and top with an even layer of mashed potatoes. Brush the potatoes with beaten egg. Bake for 20 minutes until golden and bubbling. Serve immediately.

Bag-poached salmon with fennel butter

This is another recipe I dreamed up outdoors. My number one obsession is salmon fishing and when I'm out it is usual to cook up some salmon fillets in foil in the fire for lunch. One particular day, when one of my chums had caught the perfect salmon, the foil got left behind. We did have some white wine, butter, onions and fennel, and the river banks were covered in wild chives, but no foil to cook the fish in. Given the task of solving the problem, I rooted around in the provisions bag, and found a roll of sealable plastic food bags. This recipe came to mind; it is not only a quick and easy way to cook the fish, but involves no washing up – perfect.

Serves 4

Preparation: 15 minutes

Cooking: 10–15 minutes, depending on the size of the fish

4 salmon fillets

salt and pepper

2 bulbs fennel, sliced

2 onions, peeled and sliced

4 large knobs of butter

200 ml/7 fl oz white wine

juice of 1 lemon

bunch of chives, chopped

4 sealable plastic freezer bags

Put a saucepan of water on to boil. Season each salmon fillet and place it in a bag. Add a few pieces of fennel and onion and a knob of butter to each bag. Add a splash of wine and a squeeze of lemon to each bag and seal. Cook the bags in boiling water for 10 minutes, or a little longer if the fillets are large.

Lift out the salmon and place the fish and lovely crisp fennel on the plate, then sprinkle over some chives. Eat on your lap and imagine you are by a beautiful gurgling river.

Hot smoked salmon fillets with a warm potato and mangetout salad

I pinched this recipe from a fishing guide in British Columbia, Canada, who made this for me several years ago using a wild salmon that we had caught only an hour earlier. The dark teriyaki marinade went perfectly with the fish, while the double bag smoking method impressed me beyond belief. You have to try it – this one will really impress the guests. The best heat source for this is a barbecue and you must use oakwood chippings, not fuel, for smoking.

Serves 2

Preparation: 20 minutes

Cooking: 10 minutes

thumb-sized piece fresh root ginger, peeled and finely chopped

1 garlic clove, finely chopped

1 shallot, finely chopped

1 tbsp dark, sweet soy sauce (such as Indonesian ketjap manis)

1 tbsp maple syrup

juice of 1 lime

2 x 150 g/5 oz salmon fillets

salt and freshly ground black pepper

handful of oakwood smoked chippings (available from kitchen shops)

Warm potato and mangetout salad:

325 g/11 oz new potatoes

150 g/5 oz mangetout, sliced diagonally

splash of olive oil

juice of 1 lemon and lemon wedges

knob of butter

handful each of chopped coriander and basil

salt and freshly ground black pepper

In a saucepan mix together the ginger, garlic, shallot, soy sauce, maple syrup and lime juice. Bring to the boil and reduce down to make the sticky teriyaki glaze.

Take a sheet of foil, 30 cm/12 in long. Lay the salmon fillets side by side on one half of the foil, drizzle over the glaze and season well. Fold the foil over and make it into an envelope so the salmon is completely sealed. Take another sheet of foil, sprinkle half the chippings on one half, then put the salmon parcel on top of the chippings. Use a sharp knife to prick the top of the inner bag 20 times, fold the outer foil over the top and seal it in.

Put the foil parcel on a hot griddle pan or barbecue. Smoke for about 7–10 minutes.

Meanwhile, boil the new potatoes until tender and do the same with the mangetout. Toss the potatoes with the mangetout in some olive oil, lemon juice, lemon wedges and a knob of butter. Mix in the herbs, season and serve with the salmon.

Poached smoked haddock with Savoy cabbage and pancetta

I have always had a particular fondness for smoked fish, and I think that of all the types available, haddock is my favourite. For many years now I have dabbled with smoking my own fish, and have come to the conclusion that unless you are willing to invest in a proper smoker, one that will both hot and cold smoke, there is not much point in trying to do it yourself. Having said that, I always take a little box smoker with me when I go fly fishing, as it takes only a few minutes to hot-smoke a trout perfectly. There is a world of difference between this type of crude smoking, where you are effectively oven-baking a fish with a smoke effect, and proper cold smoking. Buy only real undyed haddock for this, and get the biggest fillets you can. The sweet flaky flesh of the haddock goes perfectly with the smoky pancetta and crunchy cabbage. This takes no time to make and is a really impressive dinner party special.

Serves 2
Preparation: 15 minutes
Cooking: 25 minutes

4 slices pancetta, plus 100 g/3½ oz pancetta lardons

1 litre/1¾ pints milk

salt and pepper

2 pieces of haddock fillet, 200 g/7 oz each

25 g/1 oz butter

½ Savoy cabbage, finely sliced

1 medium onion

100 ml/3½ fl oz Fish Stock (see page 188)

100 ml/3½ fl oz white wine

50 ml/2 fl oz double cream

chopped chives, to garnish (optional)

Remove and reserve the rind from the pancetta slices, then grill them until crispy. Bring the milk to the boil and add seasoning and the rind from the pancetta. Turn the heat down to a simmer and add the haddock. Cook for 6–7 minutes, then remove from the heat.

In another pan, sweat the finely sliced cabbage and onion and pancetta lardons in a little butter. Season and cook for 2 minutes. Add the fish stock and white wine to the pan and cook until the liquid is reduced by half . Now add the cream and reduce a little more. Spoon the cabbage mixture into two bowls, lay the haddock fillets on top, and spoon the remaining sauce around. Garnish with the pancetta slices. A few chopped chives make a good garnish.

Warm potato and fennel salad with grilled mackerel

Mackerel is one of the most evocative fish of my childhood. As a kid we used to go on holiday to the seaside, to places like Devon and Sussex on England's southern coastline. I used to throw lines off the rocks baited with hooks and coloured feathers, and I remember my astonishment and delight when a bright striped mackerel came wriggling out of the water. Nowadays, I often go sea fishing with friends, and am always happiest when we decide that the afternoon's quarry will be mackerel. Always make this recipe with the freshest mackerel, ones that have shiny skin, bright eyes, and no smell.

Serves 2
Preparation: 10–15 minutes
Cooking: 20 minutes

2 fresh mackerel, filleted
salt and pepper
zest and juice of 1 lemon
a glug of olive oil

Potato and fennel salad:
625 g/1¼ lb new potatoes
1 tsp wholegrain mustard
1 tbsp white wine vinegar
1 large fennel bulb, finely sliced
1 red onion, finely sliced
small bunch of flat-leaf parsley, chopped

Preheat the grill to hot. Season the mackerel well, squeeze a few drops of lemon juice and a sprinkling of zest over each, and dribble them with olive oil. Place under the hot grill skin-side up. After 5 minutes, turn them over for 5 minutes to brown the meat, which will be nearly cooked by now. Set aside to rest.

To make the salad, boil the potatoes until firm but cooked, and cut them in half. Put them in a mixing bowl with a splash of olive oil, the rest of the lemon juice and zest, and the mustard and vinegar. Mix well, then add the fennel and onion. Now throw in a good amount of parsley and season well.

Scoop a mound of salad into bowls, lay the mackerel fillets on top, and pour over the juices from the bottom of the mixing bowl. Chilled rosé wine or cider are ideal accompanying drinks.

A rich, oily fish stew

This is a general dish, the sort of thing you will get plonked in front of you in a little bar or café anywhere in Mediterranean France, Spain and Italy.
I would serve this in a copper pan, with some really good bread, and a bottle of good chilled Sauvignon Blanc. Remember, you can play around with dishes like this, as long as the basic principles of stock, saffron and tomatoes are adhered to.

Serves 4
Preparation: 15 minutes
Cooking: 25 minutes

125 ml/4 fl oz good quality olive oil

1 bulb of fennel, roughly sliced

3 garlic cloves, peeled and chopped

1 onion, sliced

2 carrots, diced

24 cherry tomatoes

1 glass white wine

1 litre/1¾ pints Fish Stock (see page 188)

a pinch of saffron

4 hake steaks

4 small red mullet

2 handfuls of mussels

12 small clams

8 large raw prawns, in their shells

a splash of pastis

salt and pepper

If you have one, use a copper pan for this; if not, then a good deep casserole dish will work, or a heavy cast-iron pan. Pour the oil into the pan, and add the fennel, garlic, onion and carrot. Soften for a few minutes then add the tomatoes, squashing each as you add it to the pan.

Cook for a minute or two more, then add the wine. Cook for 2 minutes, then add the fish stock. Add the saffron, and stir well. The stew should be just at simmering point.

Now add the hake, gently pushing the fish under the surface. Next the mullet, slashed on each side a couple of times. Cook the fish for 4–5 minutes, then add the mussels, prawns and clams. These will open and add their juices to the stew. Cook for 5 minutes, check the seasoning, and add a splash of pastis. Give the stew 3 minutes more for luck and bring to the table. I like to lift the lid off in front of the guests, as it never fails to get an 'ooohh', thus satisfying my fragile ego.

Trout in newspaper with mash and parsley sauce

I quite often cook up a trout on the riverbank when fly fishing. The beauty of this dish is that you can do it posh-style in the oven with the mash and sauce, or over the coals of a campfire, just with bread and mayonnaise.

Serves 2

Preparation: 20 minutes

Cooking: 20–30 minutes, depending on the size of the trout

2 sheets of newspaper

1 trout, whole but gutted

2 bay leaves

1 lemon, sliced

25 g/1 oz butter

salt and pepper

Sauce:

200 g/7 oz butter, cut into 1 cm/½ in cubes

2 shallots, finely chopped

½ glass dry white wine

zest and juice of 1 lemon

1 tbsp flat-leaf parsley, finely chopped

salt and pepper

Mash:

500 g/1 lb potatoes (preferably King Edward)

1 tbsp wholegrain mustard

50 g/2 oz butter

50 ml/2 fl oz double cream

2 tbsp flat-leaf parsley, chopped

Soak the newspapers thoroughly in water and preheat the oven to 180°C/350°F/Gas Mark 4. If you do this on the barbecue or over the fire, make sure the newspaper is soaked through first. Don't worry if the outer layers burn, as the inner layers will protect the fish. Lay the trout on one side of the newspaper, and stuff it with the bay leaves, lemon slices, and a few dots of butter. Season well, and wrap up in the newspaper. Place in the oven for 30 minutes.

Meanwhile, put the potatoes for the mash on to boil and make the sauce. Cook the shallots in a dot of butter until they are softened, then add the wine, lemon juice and zest. Reduce by two-thirds, and turn the heat right down. Add the remaining butter piece by piece until the sauce emulsifies into a beautiful thick, glossy concoction. Add the parsley and season to taste.

When the potatoes are cooked, drain them and add the remaining mash ingredients. Beat until smooth and rich.

Remove the trout from the oven and cut open the parcel. The skin should stick to the paper, leaving the perfectly cooked fillets behind. Lay a fillet on a pile of mash and top with the butter sauce.

Seared yellow fin tuna with chilli tomato dressing

I am possibly unusual among chefs in that I am not a huge fan of tuna. Having said that, there are two ways in which I really love it. One is in big, rare chunks in a salade Niçoise, the other is like this.

Make the marinade by mixing together the thyme, lemon juice, garlic and olive oil. Rub the tuna steaks with the marinade and set aside for 20 minutes.

Meanwhile, make the dressing. Place the sugar and water in a small saucepan and heat gently, stirring often, until dissolved into a syrup. In a blender, blend together the chopped tomatoes and chilli. Sieve the tomato purée into a saucepan. Add the sugar syrup. Cook briskly, stirring often until reduced to a thick syrup. Set aside to cool.

Make the salsa by mixing together the tomatoes, rocket, capers and parsley.

Preheat a griddle or frying pan until very hot. Place the tuna on the hot pan and cook for 2 minutes on either side.

To serve, place each griddled tuna steak in the centre of a plate. Spoon most of the tomato dressing over the tuna steaks. Spoon the marinade and the remaining dressing round the edge of the plates. Top the tuna with the salsa.

Serves 2

Preparation: 30 minutes, plus marinating

Cooking: 10 minutes

2 large tuna steaks, about 150 g/5 oz each

Marinade:
1 tsp chopped thyme
juice of 1 lemon
2 garlic cloves, finely crushed
1 tsp olive oil

Dressing:
100 g/3½ oz sugar
100 ml/3½ fl oz water
1 x 400 g/13 oz can chopped tomatoes
1 red chilli, deseeded and chopped
salt and freshly ground pepper

Salsa:
4 fresh plum tomatoes, finely chopped
1 bunch rocket, finely chopped
1 tbsp capers, finely chopped
1 bunch flat-leaf parsley, finely chopped

Moroccan-style stuffed sardines

Sardines have long been regarded as the cheapest and nastiest fish in the seas, but they are now enjoying a long-awaited comeback. For me sardines conjure up images of childhood holidays to Portugal and Greece, where driftwood barbecues would grill dozens of fresh silvery sardines that needed just a squeeze of lemon and some olive oil to create the perfect lunch.

Serves 2
Preparation: 30 minutes
Cooking: 20 minutes

6 sardines, gutted and heads removed but left in one piece

olive oil, for rubbing

sea salt and freshly ground black pepper

Gremolata:

zest and juice of 2 lemons

2 cloves garlic, chopped

1 handful flat-leaf parsley, chopped

1 tsp capers, chopped

2 tbsp olive oil

Couscous:

500 ml/17 fl oz Chicken Stock (see page 187)

pinch of saffron

100 g/3½ oz couscous

zest and juice of 1 lemon

2 tbsp olive oil

½ red pepper, roasted and skinned, then diced small

1 tbsp chopped mint

1 tbsp chopped basil

Salsa:

2 ripe plum tomatoes concasse (skinned and finely diced)

25 g/1 oz green olives, chopped

1 tbsp capers

2 anchovies, chopped

½ red pepper, roasted and skinned, then diced small

juice of ½ lemon

2 tbsp olive oil

1 tbsp chopped mint

½ red chilli, deseeded and finely chopped

To start, roast 1 red pepper, then skin and dice finely. Use half for the Couscous and half for the Salsa.

Lay the sardines cavity-side down and gently thump them along the backbone with a wooden spoon. Turn them over and the whole backbone and ribcage should pull out, leaving a perfect double fillet. Make the gremolata by mixing together all the ingredients, then use it to stuff the sardines. Tie each one up with pieces of cotton string, rub with olive oil, sprinkle with sea salt and black pepper, and place on a medium-hot griddle pan. Cook for 5 minutes on each side.

Meanwhile, prepare the couscous. Heat up the chicken stock and stir in the saffron. When it is boiling, pour it over the couscous, stir well and cover. Leave for 6 minutes, then add the other ingredients. Season well.

For the salsa, simply mix the ingredients together and season to taste.

To serve, artfully pile the couscous on the plate, then lay the sardines on the couscous (you can snip the string off first, or leave it for your guests to do). Spoon the salsa around the plate and serve.

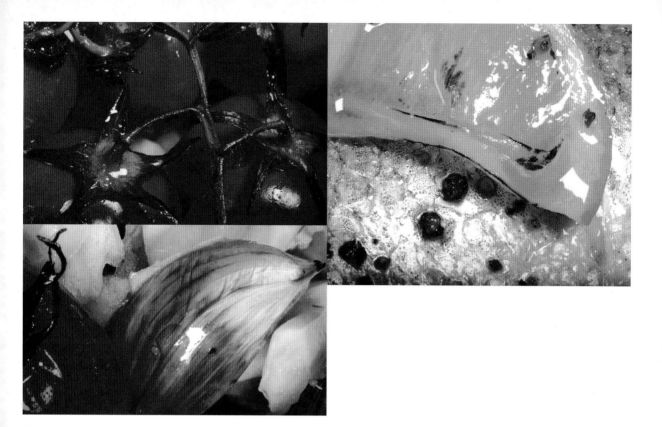

Seabass baked with rosemary and fennel

I love cooking fish like this. The flavour of the herbs gently infuses the fish, without overpowering it. You can do this with any good-sized fish.

Serves 2

Preparation: 5 minutes

Cooking: 25 minutes

1 whole seabass, about 750 g/1½ lb, gutted

large bunch of rosemary sprigs

6 garlic cloves, unpeeled

2 fennel bulbs, sliced

50 ml/2 fl oz olive oil

sea salt and pepper

juice of 2 unwaxed lemons (keep the squeezed halves)

1 glass white wine

2 or 3 bunches cherry tomatoes on the vine

Preheat the oven to 220°C/425°F/Gas Mark 7. Slash the sides of the fish 3 or 4 times on each side. Next lay half the rosemary on the bottom of a roasting tray, along with the garlic cloves and fennel slices and pour half the olive oil over them. Sit the fish on the fennel and garlic and season it with sea salt and pepper.

Place the remaining rosemary on top and around the fish and drench the whole affair with the lemon juice, wine and remaining olive oil. This will hopefully stop the rosemary burning. Arrange the cherry tomatoes on the vine around the fish. Add the squeezed lemons to the pan. Roast in the oven for 20 minutes. Halfway through, baste the fish with the pan juices.

Rest the fish for 3 minutes before serving. Strain the pan juices through a sieve and pour over the fish for a wonderful sauce. Serve with a crisp green salad.

game

introduction

Thanks to a long tradition of shooting, throughout the year there is a huge amount of cheap, delicious ingredients available for those who wish to make use of them: pheasant, partridge, pigeon, rabbit, hare, ducks, geese and venison. I have a real passion for game cookery, and really believe we should make more use of what we have. There is no time in the year when game is not available, nor is it ever very expensive. A good butcher should always have a source of supply, and will always be able to procure you a couple of rabbits or some lovely wild venison, and if you ask nicely, he should be willing to prepare the game for you.

I still remember the first time I went shooting proper. I was about 13 and managed to shoot one pheasant. I was chuffed to bits, and although that was the only bird I shot that day, I was still given my ritual brace of birds at the end by the keeper. I think we hung those birds for a week in our garage, and every day was purgatory, I was so keen to get cooking. When they were pronounced ready by our elderly neighbour Archie, we plucked the pheasants, cleaned them and debated the merits of roasting versus casseroling. It was decided to give me the casting vote, as the provider. Of course the casserole won, and Archie very generously donated a bottle of his excellent claret for the cooking liquid. Some thyme from the garden, a handful of shallots and garlic, a dab of tomato purée and some fat, smoked bacon was bunged in the pot with the browned pheasant pieces, and the claret added. As far as I can remember, it was judged an unqualified success.

To this day Pheasant Casserole, rich with red wine, shallots and garlic, remains to me the most perfect of game recipes, absolutely delicious and completely satisfying.

A warm salad of pigeon and black pudding

Of all the game birds, I think pigeon is the least appreciated. The meat is rich and dark, takes seconds to cook, and tastes like a cross between the best calves' liver and good beef. You can find them now in the supermarkets, all ready to cook, you just have to watch out for the odd lead shot. This quick recipe is perfect for a good summer salad, and will take all of 5 minutes to cook.

Serves 4

Preparation: 15 minutes

Cooking: 5–10 minutes

2 tbsp olive oil

200 g/7 oz pancetta or dry-cured streaky bacon, in lardons

400 g/13 oz black pudding, sliced

4 pigeon breasts

salt and pepper

2 tbsp sherry or balsamic vinegar

juice of 1 lemon

2 large handfuls mixed peppery leaves (rocket, baby spinach, watercress)

Heat 1 tablespoon of olive oil in a pan. When this is really hot, add the pancetta or bacon and cook until they start to crisp, then remove from the heat. In another pan, do the same to the sliced black pudding. When it is crisp, crumble it into pieces and transfer the pancetta to the pudding pan. Turn down the heat.

Place the pancetta pan back on the heat and add the olive oil to the reserved fat. Season each pigeon breast and sear for 2 minutes each side. After 4 minutes, remove them, let them rest, and deglaze their cooking pan with half the sherry or balsamic vinegar. Pour and scrape the contents in with the black pudding and pancetta. Pour the rest of the sherry or vinegar over this mixture.

Dress the leaves with the remaining olive oil and the lemon juice and pile on to two plates. Spread the black pudding, pancetta and vinegar over and around, then slice the rare pigeon breasts over the salads.

Spatchcock woodpigeon

What a maligned bird the woodpigeon is! Here we
have a beautiful, plump, delicious-flavoured bird,
wild and organic in the truest sense of the word, and
we hardly touch it from a culinary point of view.

When the season is right, woodpigeon are the
farmers' curse, descending on fields in their
thousands, eating literally tons of grain. As a result, a
good pigeon shooter can shoot hundreds in a day, if he
is well-concealed and the woodies are in a feeding
frenzy. Woodpigeon are available in butchers' shops
and should be snapped up when you see them. This is
a great way of cooking woodpigeon, and perfect on
the barbecue.

Serves 4
Preparation: 25 minutes
Cooking: 20 minutes

4 woodpigeons
3 tbsp olive oil
4 garlic cloves
4 rosemary sprigs
sea salt
balsamic vinegar
1 glass red wine

First, spatchcock the pigeons. To do this, lay the pigeon on its
breast and cut either side of the backbone with heavy scissors.
Open up the pigeons and bash them a couple of times with the
heel of your hand to flatten them.

In a pestle and mortar, pound the olive oil, garlic, rosemary
needles and a little sea salt. Marinate the pigeons in the mixture
for 20 minutes. Preheat a griddle pan or frying pan and brush the
excess oil off the pigeon. Sear the pigeons for 3 minutes on each
side, until they take on a really good colour. Now pop them on the
barbecue or under the grill for 5 minutes on each side. Pour a
splash of balsamic vinegar and the red wine into the griddle pan
to deglaze the pigeon juices.

Cut each of the pigeons into 4 pieces, pile on a plate, pour over
the pan juices and serve with a rocket salad and Roasted
Rosemary Tomatoes (see page 152).

Roast partridge with game sauce and bubble and squeak

The key to this great recipe is the game stock in the Game Sauce. It takes a while, but is amazingly worthwhile. If you let the bones roast to almost burnt darkness, and then boil the stock for many happy hours, you will be left with a wonderful dark, rich liquid that will blow you away. I like to serve this sauce around the bubble and squeak and the partridge, not poured all over it. Simple but perfect, and dare I say it, very classy fare indeed. Always make more stock than you need and freeze it in small bags. There is a recipe in the back of the book for both the stock and the sauce. You can use French partridge or woodpigeon instead.

Serves 4

Preparation: 20 minutes

Cooking: 10 minutes

2 tbsp duck fat

4 English partridges

4 strips smoked streaky bacon

4 cakes of Bubble and Squeak (see page 148)

1 quantity Game Sauce (see page 185)

knob of butter

salt and pepper

Preheat the oven to 200°C/400°F/Gas Mark 6. Heat half the duck fat in an ovenproof pan until smokingly hot. Season the partridges and sear them for 1 minute on each breast. Take the pan off the heat and lay a rasher of bacon over each bird. Place the pan in the hot oven for 8 minutes (Frenchmen and pigeons take 2 minutes longer).

Meanwhile, in the remaining duck fat, cook the Bubble and Squeak. Fry it for about 5 minutes on each side until golden. Remove the birds from the oven, discard or munch the bacon and let the birds rest for 3–4 minutes. Heat up the Game Sauce and finish it with a few pieces of butter.

Now cut the breasts and the legs off the birds. Place a Bubble and Squeak in the middle of each plate, lay the breasts on top, and prop the thigh portions on either side. Spoon the sauce around the Bubble and Squeak and serve with redcurrant jelly. Fantastic!

Serves 4
Preparation: 20 minutes
Cooking: 15 minutes

4 partridge crowns (breasts still attached to the bone, but wings and legs removed)

salt and pepper

4 thyme sprigs

12 slices pancetta or smoked streaky bacon

25 g/1 oz butter, plus extra for deglazing

2 tbsp olive oil

2 onions, finely chopped

100 g/3½ oz pancetta lardons

4 garlic cloves, crushed

1 Savoy cabbage, sliced

100 ml/3½ fl oz Chicken Stock (see page 187)

200ml.7 fl oz Marsala

Partridge roast with cabbage, bacon and Marsala

Partridge is so plump and delicious that I favour it above all other game birds. There are two types of partridge in England, the English or grey partridge and the red-legged or French partridge, but greys are fairly scarce. French partridge is plump-breasted, with pale almost white flesh, mild and very juicy in flavour. The grey has dark, almost grouse-like flesh, and is very rich. As with most meats, roasting on the bone retains juiciness and flavour.

Preheat the oven to 200°C/400°F/Gas Mark 6. Season the partridge crowns and lay a sprig of thyme on each, then wrap them in 3 slices of pancetta each, securing with cotton string. Heat the butter and oil in a heavy ovenproof pan, and sear the breasts until they are a good golden colour. Remove from the pan and set aside.

In the same pan, fry the onions until beginning to soften, then add the pancetta lardons and cook until beginning to brown. Add the crushed garlic and sliced cabbage to the pan and sauté for a few minutes. Pour in the stock and lay the partridge on top of the cabbage. Cover with foil and cook in a preheated oven for 10 minutes. Remove the foil and make sure the birds are just cooked (the juices should run clear); if they are not give them 5 minutes more.

Remove the birds and cabbage from the pan and set aside to rest. Bring the pan to the heat and deglaze with a glass of Marsala. Add a knob of butter to the pan and incorporate into the wine.

To serve, pile some cabbage on a plate and lay a partridge crown on top. Pour a tablespoon or so of the intense Marsala sauce over each one and enjoy!

Hot-smoked teriyaki pheasant

I thought up this recipe a couple of years ago when having an argument with a fellow chef about pheasants. This chap was convinced that pheasants were indigenous to Europe; I was convinced that they were of Far-Eastern origin. Happily, I was proved correct and in a gloating moment made up this recipe to salute the pheasants' honourable ancestors. For this recipe you will need a box smoker, which you can buy in any good kitchen shop. Or use the double foil method described on page 66.

Serves 4

Preparation: 15 minutes, plus 2 hours' marinating

Cooking: 10 minutes

5 cm/2 in piece fresh root ginger, peeled and finely chopped

2 lemongrass stalks, peeled and chopped

4 garlic cloves, crushed

6 tbsp sweet dark soy sauce (such as Indonesian ketjap manis)

4 tbsp maple syrup

juice of 1 lime

4 pheasant breasts

salt and freshly ground pepper

250 g/8 oz egg noodles

2 tbsp sesame oil

small bunch of fresh coriander, chopped

small bunch of rocket, roughly torn

1 red chilli, deseeded and very finely chopped

In a small saucepan, mix together the ginger, lemon grass, garlic, soy sauce, maple syrup and lime juice. Bring to the boil, stirring constantly. Reduce the heat and simmer until reduced and thickened to a caramel-like consistency.

Using a sharp knife, lightly score the pheasant breasts and toss with the ginger mixture. Season with salt and pepper. Cover and marinate in the fridge for at least 2 hours. Remove the breasts and reserve the marinade. In a smoker, smoke the pheasant breasts for 10 minutes.

Meanwhile, bring a large pan of salted water to the boil. Add the noodles and cook until just softened. Drain the cooked noodles and toss with the sesame oil, fresh coriander (reserving a few leaves for the garnish), rocket and chilli. Season with salt and freshly ground pepper.

Slice the smoked pheasant breasts and serve the pheasant on top of the noodles. Drizzle the reserved marinade around the noodles and sprinkle over the reserved coriander leaves.

Old-fashioned roast brace of pheasants with bread sauce and chipolatas

Surely there is no more handsome a bird than a cock pheasant in all his scarlet and black glory. That it is also the stupidest bird imaginable is beside the point – you just know that a bird that good-looking is going to taste great. I always keep the tail feathers from these birds – I love giving them their tails back when they are served at the table, it adds real theatre to the meal and tells your guests that they are definitely not eating chicken!

Chipolatas, game sauce or gravy and bread sauce are definitely de rigueur. A really simple bread sauce takes some beating. I like to infuse the milk with some flavour first, but feel free to play with it. Don't make it too smooth in texture, it should be a bit coarse.

Serves 4–6
Preparation: 15 minutes, plus infusing
Cooking: 60–70 minutes, plus resting

2 lemons

2 rosemary sprigs

1 brace of pheasants (a cock and a hen); try to get the tail feathers.

1 tbsp duck fat

2 thyme sprigs

8 rashers streaky bacon

500 g/1 lb chipolatas

1 quanity Game Sauce or Gravy (see pages 185 and 186)

Bread sauce:
600 ml/1 pint milk

1 red onion, peeled

gratings of nutmeg

1 bay leaf

100 g/3$\frac{1}{2}$ oz white bread, crusts removed (a day or two old is good)

salt and pepper

knob of butter

Preheat the oven to 160°C/325°F/Gas Mark 3. Stuff a lemon and a sprig of rosemary into the cavity of each bird, rub them with half of the fat, then place them breast-side down on a trivet. Cover with foil and roast in a preheated oven for 40 minutes. Turn the oven up to 200°C/400°F/Gas Mark 6, and remove the birds. Turn them over, and rub the breasts with the remaining fat, then spread the thyme and bacon rashers across the breasts. Sprinkle the pan with chipolatas and roast, uncovered, for a further 20–25 minutes.

Meanwhile, make the bread sauce. Place the milk, onion, nutmeg and bay leaf in a pan. Bring the liquid to the boil, then take off the heat. Leave for a good 30 minutes. Ten minutes before serving, tear the bread into bits. Remove the onion and bay leaf from the milk and add the bread. Bring back up to heat and season. Stir for 5 minutes, then add a knob of butter if you wish.

When the birds are done, remove from the oven and rest for 10 minutes. Meanwhile, heat up the Game Sauce or Gravy. Serve the pheasants on a big platter with the chipolatas piled around and with gravy boats of bread sauce and Game Sauce or Gravy.

Gennaro's pheasant

I named this dish after my chum and Italian mentor, Gennaro Contaldo, who finally persuaded me that simplicity is what counts in cooking rustic food. This dish really allows the flavour of the pheasant to come through; don't be tempted to muck around with it too much. This is real peasant food, and needs good bread and should be eaten with your fingers! If you're squeamish, ask your butcher to prepare the hens.

Serves 4

Preparation: 15 minutes

Cooking: 20 minutes, plus 15 minutes' resting

2 pheasant hens (young if possible), backbones removed, cut in half and trimmed of any nasty bits

50 ml/2 fl oz olive oil

sea salt and freshly ground pepper

2 lemons, quartered

4 bulbs of garlic

10 large rosemary sprigs

2 glasses white wine

Place the prepared pheasants, olive oil, seasoning, and quartered lemons in a big bowl. Mix well. Squash up the garlic, but don't peel it, and add to the mix. Strip a third of the rosemary leaves off the stalks and add them too.

Preheat the oven to 230°C/450°F/Gas Mark 8. Now sear the pheasants in a hot ovenproof pan to colour. Add the rest of the rosemary, then pour over the white wine. Cover the pan with foil, and place in the oven for 20 minutes. Remove and rest the meat for 15 minutes. There should be enough pan juices for a couple of spoonfuls over each pheasant half. If not, heat up the pan, pour some more wine in and deglaze.

Serve simply with boiled or Boulangère Potatoes (see page 142) and a green salad. Some nice, oily, focaccia-style bread is particularly good for mopping up the roasting juices – try squeezing the squashed garlic onto the bread first.

Rabbit with shallots, rosemary and garlic with parsley mash

Rabbit is incredibly delicious. It is low in fat, a white meat, and does not have a strong, gamey flavour. It is also cheap to buy, and remember, a wild rabbit is organic in the true sense of the word! In my book, rabbit is superior to chicken in nearly every way and should be a lot more popular. Everyone who can make a casserole can cook rabbit successfully, which is why I've included this lovely rich rabbit stew.

Serves 8

Preparation: 1 hour

Cooking: 3 hours

1 tbsp plain flour

sea salt and freshly ground black pepper

2 large rabbits, each cut into 8 pieces (ask your butcher to do this for you)

25 g/1 oz butter

3–4 tbsp olive oil

100 g/3½ oz smoked bacon or pancetta lardons

25–30 shallots

8 garlic cloves, finely chopped (plus extra cloves peeled and left whole, optional)

2 bottles red wine (Burgundy or Pinot Noir)

2 large rosemary sprigs

2 tbsp cornflour mixed with 1 tbsp softened butter, to thicken the sauce

1 tbsp chopped parsley, to serve

Parsley mash:

2 kg/4 lb floury potatoes, such as Maris Piper or King Edward, peeled and cut into 2.5 cm/1 in chunks

large bunch of curly parsley, finely chopped

75 g/3 oz butter, softened

3–4 tbsp hot milk

salt and freshly ground black pepper

Season the flour with salt and freshly ground black pepper. Roll the joints of rabbit in the flour. Heat the butter and olive oil in a heavy casserole dish over a medium heat. Gently fry the rabbit pieces until golden brown all over (do this in batches). Remove all the rabbit pieces and reserve.

Add the bacon to the casserole dish. While that is cooking, peel the shallots. Chop half of them finely and leave the rest whole. Add them all to the bacon in the casserole, together with the garlic. Cook for 5–6 minutes, until everything is browned off and the bottom of the casserole is sticky and a bit burned (this is a good thing, I promise).

Now for the fun bit. Turn up the heat and add a glass of red wine. Scrape away at the bottom of the casserole and all the burnt bits will come away, making the beginnings of a super rich sauce.

Preheat the oven to 180°C/350°F/Gas Mark 4. Add the rabbit to the casserole, packing it in tightly. Lay the rosemary on top. If you wish, sprinkle the rabbit with more whole unpeeled garlic cloves. Add red wine until the rabbit is covered.

Cover the casserole and cook for 1½ hours for farmed rabbit, or 2½ hours if you are using wild rabbit. When the rabbit is so tender it melts off the bone, transfer the meat to a serving dish and leave the sauce in the pot.

Meanwhile, make the parsley mash. Boil the potatoes for 15–20 minutes, until tender. Drain really well, and then shake until they are dry and fluffy. Mash until smooth. Add all the chopped parsley, the butter and milk. Season well.

Place the casserole dish containing the sauce over a medium heat, stir in the cornflour and butter and continue stirring until you have a thick sauce.

Pour the sauce over the rabbit and scatter over all the gorgeous shallots and cooked garlic. Add a sprinkling of parsley and serve with the parsley mash.

Rabbit with cider, mustard and thyme

In my humble opinion, certain combinations are meant to be: fish and chips, hamburger and fries, and rabbit and mustard. Remember, this is not a casserole, it is more of a pot roast, and doesn't take all that long. Serve it with some good sauté potatoes and drink lashings of cider.

Serves 4
Preparation: 15 minutes
Cooking: 1 hour

2 wild or 1 reared rabbit, jointed into 8 pieces (ask your butcher to do this for you)

3 tbsp seasoned plain flour, for coating

4 onions

12 garlic cloves, unpeeled

50 g/2 oz butter

4 tbsp olive oil

large bunch of thyme, chopped

1.2 litres/2 pints still cider

2 tbsp wholegrain mustard

1 tbsp honey

Coat all the rabbit pieces with seasoned flour, and set aside. Roughly slice the onions and smash up the garlic a little, but do not peel it. Put the butter and oil in a large sauté pan on a high heat. When the oil/butter combination is hot, add the rabbit. Leave to brown really well, then turn over and brown the other side. Add the onion and garlic and the thyme. Cook for 10 minutes, then add the cider and mustard. Put the lid on, and simmer for 40 minutes.

At the end of this time, there should be very little juice left. Add the honey, check the rabbit is falling off the bone. Serve with sauté potatoes, a green salad and a bottle of good cider. Perfection!

Jugged hare

Records of this recipe have been found as far back as the eighth century. It features early in my culinary history too: it was the second game recipe I ever cooked. You may think it peculiar that this recipe includes so many exotic spices, like cloves and allspice, but remember, hares were royal animals in the Middle Ages and spices were their way of showing how posh, rich and sophisticated they were.

In the old days, blood from the hare was a crucial ingredient, added to thicken and flavour the sauce. You can use chicken livers instead, finely chopped or whizzed quickly in a blender.

Make sure you feel the hare's bum before you buy it! A lot of hares unfortunately get shot in the derriere, which ruins the best meat. Best of all is a rifle-shot hare as this will have not damaged the meaty bits.

Serves 4–6

Preparation: 1 hour, plus overnight marinating

Cooking: 3 hours

Marinade:

150 ml/¼ pint red wine

3 cloves

1 bay leaf

½ tsp allspice

Jugged hare:

1 hare, preferably not too old, jointed into 8 or 10 pieces

3 tbsp seasoned plain flour, for coating

1 tbsp duck fat

1 bouquet garni

125 g/4 oz bacon lardons

2 onions, chopped

3 cloves

½ tsp allspice, ground

zest of 1 lemon

salt and freshly ground black pepper

1 litre/1¾ pints Chicken Stock (see page 187)

25 g/1 oz butter

25 g/1 oz plain flour

125 g/4 oz chicken livers, finely chopped

50 ml/2 fl oz tbsp red wine

50 ml/2 fl oz port

2 tbsp redcurrant jelly

Mix all the marinade ingredients together. Place the hare pieces in a non-metallic bowl and pour over the marinade. Leave for several hours, or overnight if possible. Remove the pieces from the marinade and pat dry with kitchen paper. Lightly coat the joints with the seasoned flour.

Preheat the oven to 160°C/325°F/Gas Mark 3. Melt the duck fat in a frying pan and cook the hare pieces on all sides to seal. Transfer them to a casserole dish. Add the herbs, bacon, onion, cloves, allspice, lemon zest and a little of the marinade. Season and then cover with the chicken stock, and bring to the boil. Transfer to the oven and cook for 2½ hours, or until tender. Remove the hare, onions and bacon with a slotted spoon and keep hot on a warmed serving dish. Remove and discard the bouquet garni and the cloves from the cooking liquid.

In a small saucepan, melt the butter and stir in the flour. Add the butter-flour mix to the cooking liquid bit by bit, so it does not become too thick. Stir in the chopped chicken livers, wine, port, and the redcurrant jelly. Mix well and adjust the seasoning if necessary.

Pour the sauce over the hare and serve with extra redcurrant jelly if desired. I think this is best served with boiled or mashed potatoes and good bread.

Carpaccio of roe-deer fillet

There are few lovelier animals than the shy and elusive roe-deer. You will find the venison from a roe much superior to that of a heavier red deer and much less overpowering in taste. Ask your butcher to get it for you to ensure the animal is bought from a licensed stalker or gamekeeper. There is a problem with poached wild deer, which all too often will not have been properly treated after shooting. The rule of thumb I would follow is this: don't buy roe meat that is very dark and blood- coloured – it is probably poached. A good piece of roe should be a sort of pinkish colour, almost veal-like. This recipe uses fillet since it tastes out of this world and, unlike beef, is definitely the best cut – full of flavour. Prepared like this, it makes the perfect summer lunch.

Serves 6

Preparation: 1 hour, plus marinating

Cooking: 20 minutes

small bunches of sage, rosemary and thyme

3 garlic cloves

3 tbsp olive oil

12 dried juniper berries

1 roe-deer fillet, about 750 g/1½ lb, trimmed

500 g/1 lb cherry tomatoes on the vine

sea salt and pepper

200 g/7 oz rocket

1 tbsp sherry vinegar

Parmesan cheese, for shavings

Finely chop the herbs and garlic and pummel in a pestle and mortar with a good glug of olive oil. Add the juniper berries and give them a good squish. Rub the mixture into the trimmed fillet of venison, and leave for 1 hour. Reserve the rest of the marinade.

Preheat the oven to 200°C/400°F/Gas Mark 6. Heat a heavy pan until it is positively incandescent, and cut the venison into 2 so it will fit. Sear the venison for a minute and a half on each side, 3 minutes in all, and remove.

Put the cherry tomatoes into the pan, and pour over the rest of the herb marinade. Season, then roast the tomatoes in the oven for 12 minutes, just to start them cooking. Take the tomatoes out of the oven, and allow to cool a little.

Dress the rocket leaves with olive oil and sherry vinegar and pile in the middle of a big platter. Now thinly slice the venison and arrange around the leaves. Pile up the tomatoes on the side opposite the meat. Throw some Parmesan shavings over the salad, rip up some good bread, and have plenty of extra oil on the table.

Coarse country game terrine

At the end of every day's shooting there are always a few birds that are a little mangled, usually by an over-zealous labrador. I have a standing order with the local gamekeeper that I will take all of these birds off his hands whenever possible. With just a little bit of work these rejects, which the butcher would turn his nose up at, can be made into the most delicious terrine. I always have one in the fridge, which combined with some salad leaves and a little chutney makes the best impromptu lunch ever.

Serves 8

Preparation: 25 minutes

Cooking: 1½ hours, plus 24 hours' standing time

1 rabbit, taken off the bone and chopped into pieces

1 pheasant, taken off the bone and chopped into pieces

200 g/7 oz pork fat (available from good butchers)

200 g/7 oz diced pork shoulder

2 garlic cloves

2 tbsp chopped thyme

salt and pepper

bay leaves

juniper berries

Preheat the oven to 160°C/325°F/Gas Mark 3.

Simply whiz all the ingredients up in a food processor until the mixture has a coarse consistency, then pour into a terrine mould or small loaf tin. Cover with a sheet of baking parchment, then foil. Place the terrine in the middle of a roasting tin with 2.5 cm/1 in of hot water in the bottom and cook in the oven for 90 minutes.

Remove the terrine from the oven and allow to cool a little. Cut a piece of cardboard to fit inside the terrine and wrap in foil. Place the board on top of the terrine, pile some heavy tins on top. The idea is to compress the terrine while it is still hot to condense the contents. Leave the terrine for 24 hours before serving, decorated with bay leaves and juniper berries.

Mutton, rabbit and venison pudding

Once in a blue moon I love cooking a real old-fashioned suet pudding, one that takes 3 hours to cook and really warms the cockles of the heart. I do this instead of the old stager, Steak and Kidney, because I love the flavours of the three meats together and hate slow-cooked kidney with a passion. If you cannot get mutton, use well-matured lamb. Please use proper beef suet for this, not the veggie alternative. If you are cooking something this carnivorous, you're hardly likely to be vegetarian.

Serves 6

Preparation 30 minutes, plus 2 hours' resting time

Cooking: 3 hours

Pastry:

400 g/13 oz self-raising flour

salt and ground white pepper

200 g/7 oz shredded beef suet

water, to form paste

Filling:

2 tbsp seasoned plain flour

200 g/7 oz mutton leg, cut into 2.5 cm/1 in cubes

200 g/7 oz venison leg, cut into 2.5 cm/1 in cubes

1 rabbit, de-boned and roughly cut up

1 large onion, sliced

1 tbsp ketchup

2 thyme sprigs, chopped

1 tbsp Worcestershire sauce

200 ml/7 fl oz Game Stock, reduced by half (see page 184)

First, make the pastry. Sift the flour with a large pinch of salt and pepper into a bowl and add the suet. Mix the suet and flour together by rubbing them between your hands. When the mix looks vaguely crumby start adding water, using a knife to combine everything. When it starts to come together, use your hands; you want a silky firm paste that leaves the bowl clean. Wrap in clingfilm and leave in the fridge for at least 2 hours.

Roll all the meat in the seasoned flour. Place the meat in a bowl with the onion, ketchup, thyme and Worcestershire sauce. Season lightly.

Cut off one-quarter of the pastry and reserve it for a lid. Roll out the rest of the pastry to a thickness of 5 mm/¼ in or so and line a greased 1.8 litre/3 pint pudding mould. Make sure the pastry hangs over the edge by about 3.5 cm/1½ in. Now spoon in the meat and onions, and pour in the reduced stock. The meat should come to the very top of the basin. Roll out and lay the pastry lid on top, then crimp the edges shut, cutting off any excess. (Dampen the edge of the pastry first to ensure a good seal.) Cover with a sheet of foil pleated in the middle, to allow for expansion of the pudding during cooking. Tie the foil in place with string, including a loop over the top to act as a handle.

Steam the pudding in a casserole dish large enough to take the pudding basin and with a tight-fitting lid. Fill the bottom third of the dish with water, and put something in the bottom to act as a trivet. Steam for 3 hours, topping up with water as necessary. Uncover, up-end onto a plate and serve to an admiring audience.

Stuffed roasted saddle of venison with spiced red cabbage and port sauce

This recipe is a little fiddly, and takes a while to prepare, but is definitely worth it if you want to do an impressive dinner. I would happily serve this up as an alternative to turkey at Christmas. I prefer to use roe deer for this, but fallow is fine if roe is hard to find.

Serves 8

Preparation: 45 minutes

Cooking: venison 50 minutes, cabbage 1½ hours

Cabbage:

½ red cabbage, finely sliced

1 onion, chopped

1 apple, peeled and chopped

1 tbsp butter

6 juniper berries

2 tbsp malt vinegar

2 tbsp caster sugar

1 tsp cinnamon

salt and pepper

Venison:

1 saddle of venison, about 1.5-2 kg/3-4 lb, boned with the 2 fillets left attached to the thin layer of meat over the back and the ribs (this is needed to roll the joint up)

500 g/1 lb pork sausagemeat

1 onion, finely diced

2 tbsp sage, chopped

2 tbsp rosemary, chopped

2 garlic cloves, chopped

50 g/2 oz redcurrants

1 tbsp wholegrain mustard

2 tbsp goose fat

salt and pepper

2 tbsp chopped thyme

Sauce:

250 ml/8 fl oz port

250 ml/8 fl oz Game or dark Beef Stock (see page 184)

1 tbsp redcurrant jelly

25 g/1 oz butter

First prepare the cabbage. In a heavy pan, sauté the cabbage, onion and apple in butter for 5 minutes. Add the other ingredients, cover and cook on a low heat for 1½ hours. Season to taste.

Next, the venison. Preheat the oven to 200°C/400°F/Gas Mark 6. Mix the sausagemeat, onion, sage, rosemary, garlic, redcurrants and mustard together and roll out into a long sausage. Lie this down the middle of the meat, between the two fillets of venison. Wrap the flaps of venison fillet around the sausage and tie with string every 5 cm/2 in or so. Rub with the goose fat, season and sprinkle with the chopped thyme. Sear all over in a hot dry pan, then roast in the oven for 20 minutes. Rest for at least 10 minutes.

Meanwhile, make the sauce. Simply combine the port and stock in a saucepan, bring to the boil and reduce by two-thirds. Add the redcurrant jelly and finish by whisking in the butter. Carve the venison into 1 cm/½ in slices and serve on a bed of cabbage. Spoon plenty of sauce around the meat and tuck in.

Game pie

Game pie is a heroic pastry crust filled to the brim with strongly flavoured ingredients. No shooting season is complete without the ritual of a Game Pie washed down with gallons of good Bordeaux. If you can wait, all game pies are best after a day or two.

Serves at least 8

Preparation: 1 hour

Cooking: 1½ hours, plus cooling and setting

Pastry:

250 g/8 oz lard

300 ml/½ pint water

875 g/1¾ lb plain flour, plus extra for dusting

pinch of salt

butter, for greasing

Filling:

500 g/1 lb wild venison

1 rabbit, deboned

1 pheasant, off the bone

4 woodpigeon breasts

3 onions, sliced

6 garlic cloves, chopped

bunch of thyme

4 tbsp duck fat, melted

salt and freshly ground black pepper

100 g/3½ oz pancetta or smoked bacon, sliced

zest and juice of 1 lemon

1 egg, beaten

1 litre/1¾ pints Game Stock (see page 184)

5 leaves of gelatine, soaked in cold water

200 g/7 oz redcurrants

50 g/2 oz sugar

½ glass of dessert wine, preferably Sauternes

First, make the pastry by bringing the lard and water to the boil in a pan. Sift the flour into a food processor and add the salt. While the processor is on, pour the hot water and lard onto the flour and blend until you have a smooth dough. When finished, turn the dough out into a large bowl and leave to cool slightly.

Lightly butter a 15–20 cm/6–8 in pie dish or spring-formed cake tin. On a lightly floured surface, roll out two-thirds of the pastry to a thickness of about 5mm/¼in and then use it to line the pie dish, leaving an overhang. Place in the fridge to set for 30 minutes. Keep the remaining pastry covered and warm.

Preheat the oven to 200°C/400°F/Gas Mark 6. Keeping them separate, coarsely chop the venison, rabbit, pheasant and pigeon into 1 cm/½ in dice. Into each add some onion, garlic and thyme, and a tablespoon of melted duck fat. Season well.

Lay the slices of pancetta across the bottom of the pastry shell. Then add the venison, packing it in fairly tightly. Mix the lemon juice and zest with the rabbit, then add to the pie dish. Finally mix the pigeon with the pheasant and add these. The meat should come to just below the top of the dish.

Once you have filled the pie, roll out the remaining pastry on a lightly floured surface, using a little extra flour if sticky. Lay it on top of the pie, then trim and crimp the edges with your thumbs. Brush the top with some of the beaten egg.

Cut a hole in the top about 2.5 cm/1 in around then bake for 45 minutes, checking to make sure it does not burn. After this time, take the pie out of the dish and brush the sides with beaten egg. Continue baking on a baking sheet for a further 45 minutes. Leave to cool completely (overnight, if possible).

Heat the Game Stock and add the gelatine leaves, making sure they dissolve completely. Pour the stock mixture into the pie via the hole in the top. Allow the gelatine to set for at least 4 hours in the fridge.

Meanwhile, mix the redcurrants with the sugar and wine in a pan. Cook for 5 minutes over a medium heat, then leave to cool. Serve the sauce with the Game Pie.

poultry

introduction

Chicken has to be just about the most popular meat on the planet. It is cheap, readily available, quick to cook and generally tasteless, which makes it perfect for drenching in ready-made sauces and eating by the ton. This has all come about relatively recently. As little as 40 years ago a chicken was a treat for the family, only to be eaten when the bird had stopped laying eggs. The average supermarket chicken today is a mere shadow of the real thing: a watery, flavourless product of the intensive farming industry. Happily, things are getting better for the poor chicken; people are now starting to demand more flavour, and increasingly producers are leaving intensive rearing methods behind and going for quality rather than quantity.

Of course, it is possible to get really flavoursome chickens. All free-range birds will have a decent flavour because they've had a chance to develop some muscle tone and feed on some interesting and natural foods. Organic chickens will have been fed on only the best organic corn, and will have a wonderful buttery yellow colour to their skin. Always look for a fairly lean chicken, with pronounced but well-defined breasts and lean thighs. If your chicken looks like an avian Pamela Anderson, don't buy it. Go for something half the size and twice as expensive, it will be worth it.

Also included in this chapter are recipes for duck, goose, guinea fowl, cockerel and poussin.

Chicken and pumpkin soup

This recipe, not surprisingly, was invented for Halloween. I was asked to submit a recipe for a TV show, using pumpkin BUT not a plain soup, or a pie, or roasted puréed pumpkin or pumpkin risotto, because they had all been done before. Sometimes you have to really use your imagination and happily, this time it worked out well. This dish is perfect for a light meal on a cold autumnal evening.

Serves 4
Preparation: 25 minutes
Cooking: 30 minutes

1 tbsp vegetable oil

1 onion, chopped

250 g/8 oz chicken breast fillet, cubed

500 g/1 lb pumpkin, cut into chunks

salt and freshly ground pepper

100 g/3½ oz bacon lardons

500 ml/17 fl oz Chicken Stock (see page 187)

300 g/10 oz potatoes, peeled and cubed

500 ml/17 fl oz full-fat milk

500 ml/17 fl oz single cream

2 tbsp cornflour

1 tbsp chives, chopped

Heat the oil in a large saucepan. Add the onion, chicken and pumpkin and fry, stirring often, until the chicken has whitened. Season with salt and freshly ground pepper and add the bacon lardons, frying for 2–3 minutes.

Pour in the stock and add the potatoes. Bring to the boil, reduce the heat and simmer for 10–15 minutes, until the pumpkin is tender but not falling apart.

Mix the milk and cream together and combine with the cornflour. Pour the milk mixture into the pumpkin mixture and simmer for 10 minutes until the liquid is hot and thick.

Pour the soup into a large serving bowl, or for a seasonal touch, the hollowed-out pumpkin shell or small squash shells. Sprinkle with chives and serve with crusty bread rolls.

Chicken livers in red wine

This probably ranks as my number one starter. It is so easy to do, costs next to nothing, and is perfectly delicious. Keep it simple, and just serve the pink juicy livers on some olive oil toast. Make sure that you soak the livers in milk for a few hours, to remove the bitterness, then cut out the bile ducts (the green bits in the middle of the livers).

Serves 4

Preparation: 10 minutes, plus soaking

Cooking: 5–10 minutes

4 slices oily type bread, such as ciabatta

1 garlic clove, cut in half

olive oil, for drizzling

450 g/14½ oz chicken livers, soaked in milk and green bits removed

1 tbsp seasoned plain flour

50 g/2 oz butter, in small lumps

4 shallots, finely chopped

200 ml/7 fl oz red wine

1 tsp ketchup

chopped flat-leaf parsley, to garnish (optional)

salt and pepper

Preheat the oven or the grill to medium-hot and heat a heavy iron skillet, until it is smoking hot. Rub the bread with the cut garlic, and drizzle liberally with olive oil. Bake in the oven or under the grill until golden brown. Place one slice on each plate. Meanwhile, cut the livers into 2, dredge them in the seasoned flour, and shake off the excess.

Now work very quickly – the whole dish will take less than 3 minutes from this point. Throw the butter into the pan, immediately followed by the chopped shallots. Stir the shallots vigorously for a few seconds, during which time the butter will go brown and smell deliciously nutty (chefs call this stage beurre noisette). As soon as this happens, add the livers, making sure they are not crowded (it is better to do this in two batches than crowd the pan).

Cook the livers for 1 minute on each side in the foaming butter, not moving them around too much. Now pour in the red wine, which will instantly thicken because of the flour, and the ketchup, and shake the pan to mix everything together. Season and pour over the toast slices. A little chopped parsley can help finish the dish. If done correctly, the livers should be crunchy on the outside and pink in the middle, with a thick red-wine sauce.

Basque chicken

What a great recipe this is. I first had this in a tiny hotel in the Pyrenees where you didn't get a choice for dinner, but took what was given. There were no complaints from two soggy hikers (my wife and I) when we were given a cast-iron pan full of glorious Poulet Basquaise: golden chicken pieces on the bone cooked with garlic, peppers and bits of local air-dried ham. On the side was a simple dish of tomatoes and onions cooked together and the whole dish was served with a bottle of quite stunningly rough red wine and chunks of coarse brown bread. Those crazy Basques really know how to cook – this is one of the great dishes of Europe.

Serves 4

Preparation: 20 minutes

Cooking: 1½ hours

1 plump chicken, about 1.5 kg/3 lb

125 ml/4 fl oz olive oil

2 fairly hot chillis, red or green, deseeded and chopped

4 red peppers, deseeded and coarsely sliced

200 g/7 oz air-dried ham chunks (Ask your deli to slice prosciutto really thick – 5 mm/¼ in, then cut it into chunks yourself. Even better, get the shank of the prosciutto and hack it up – you can often get these free.)

1 garlic bulb, unpeeled and squashed

100 ml/3½ fl oz white wine

500 g/1 lb onions, sliced

500 g/1 lb ripe tomatoes, chopped and deseeded or 1 x 400 g/13 oz can tomatoes

salt and pepper

Start by cutting that lovely bird into 8 good pieces, then season liberally. Take your best cast-iron pan and heat 100 ml/3½ fl oz of olive oil, then add the chicken. Cook for a good 5–6 minutes on each side to brown, then add the chilli, pepper slices, ham chunks and squashed garlic. Pack everything in and don't worry about filling up the pan. Add the white wine at this point, then cover.

Turn down the heat and cook for about 1 hour. Move the chicken around every now and then to prevent things from burning and keep the heat down. The peppers will take on a glorious colour and the chicken will cook to golden perfection.

Once your chicken is going, heat up another pan and add the rest of the olive oil. Add the sliced onions and sauté until they are really soft – almost melted, in fact. Add the chopped, deseeded tomatoes (or a can of tomatoes). Turn the heat down and let time work its magic for about 20 minutes. Season to taste.

To serve, spoon the tomato and onion mix onto the plate and pile the chicken and peppers on top. Serve with big chunks of bread to mop up the golden oil.

Coq au vin

I had huge doubts about including France's finest regional speciality, because of the terrible things that are regularly done to it outside France. Now I am not a food snob, but I do think that a perfect dish – and without a doubt, a good Coq au Vin is as close to perfection as it's possible to get – should be done right or not at all. Traditionally this recipe uses a cockerel, not a chicken, and the wine must be Pinot Noir. (I will soften my puritan stance and say that a really old boiler hen will work and give a hint of the flavour of cockerel.) The other ingredients are open to debate, but basically will include smoked bacon lardons, baby onions or shallots, garlic, and possibly mushrooms, although here I leave them out.

Serves 6

Preparation: 1 hour

Cooking: 2–3 hours

50 g/2 oz flour

1 cockerel, or an old boiler hen, jointed into 12 pieces (In the UK, your butcher can get a cockerel for you. They will come from France, and he will have to order 6 at a time. If you have the freezer space, buy 6 and freeze them.)

1 tbsp duck fat

50 g/2 oz butter

24 small shallots or baby onions, peeled

4 garlic cloves, unpeeled

200 g/7 oz dry-cured smoked bacon lardons (pancetta will do, or real French poitrine fumé)

1 tsp tomato purée

1–2 bottles Pinot Noir wine

3 thyme sprigs

salt and pepper to taste

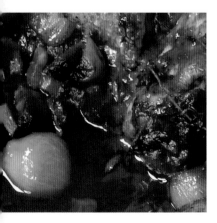

Season the flour with salt and pepper and coat the pieces of cockerel or hen, reserving the rest of the flour. Heat the duck fat and half the butter in a large, heavy casserole. When the fat is hot, cook the bird pieces on each side until a glorious golden-brown crust has formed on both sides; do it in 2 batches and don't try to hurry this stage. Now remove the bird and put to one side.

In the same pan, adding in a little more duck fat and butter if necessary, put the shallots or onions. Stir well, and add the garlic cloves, having bashed them just a little first. Now add the bacon and cook until all the ingredients start to colour.

Now comes the point where I will be accused of heresy. Add the purée, and stir in well. Return the meat to the pan and mix well. Pour over enough Pinot Noir to cover, add the thyme and put the lid on.

Preheat the oven to 160°C/325°F/Gas Mark 3. Bring the liquid in the casserole to a simmer, then cook in the oven for about 3 hours. Check after 2 hours that it is not falling apart. Remember, a chicken will cook in about an hour, so if you are using one, be careful.

When the meat is gloriously tender, lift it out of the casserole into a big earthenware bowl, cover with foil, and put the pot of sauce back on the heat. Bring it to a simmer. Rub the remaining butter with a tablespoon or two of the leftover seasoned flour. Stir into the sauce to thicken it, but make sure it dissolves properly. Check the seasoning, then pour the sauce over the meat, making sure you get all the bits of shallot, bacon and garlic. Serve with bread and boiled, buttered new potatoes.

Foil-baked chicken breasts with leeks, sage and mustard

This is the sort of thing that I cook when I have friends for lunch and can't be bothered to do anything long-winded. Cooking en papilotte, or in a bag, keeps the chicken very moist and tender, and all the other ingredients cook without losing any flavour. Leeks and mustard, of course, go very well together.

Serves 4
Preparation: 20 minutes
Cooking: 20 minutes

4 chicken breasts
4 tsp wholegrain mustard
salt and pepper
2 leeks, sliced
1 garlic clove, chopped
4 slices of prosciutto
50 g/2 oz butter
1 glass white wine
12 sage leaves
4 x 25 cm/10 in square pieces of foil

Preheat the oven to 200°C/400°F/Gas Mark 6. Rub the breasts with the mustard and season. On each piece of foil, put half a sliced leek, and a little chopped garlic. Wrap each of the mustardy breasts in a slice of prosciutto, and place on the bed of leeks. Dot the top of the chicken with butter and splash some wine over each. Place 3 sage leaves on top of each piece. Wrap the foil round each breast to make a loose but well-sealed bag; you don't want any of the juices to escape.

Bake in the oven for 20 minutes. Open the bags and plonk each one onto a plate. Mashed potato is probably my favourite thing to go with this.

Poached chicken in lemon, thyme and olive oil

The most memorable picnic I ever had was in the French Alps. Patrick, the chef from the restaurant where I was working, joined us for the day's skiing with the picnic he had prepared. When we came to the picnic site, we all knew our roles: one person got out a snow shovel and cut out a table, another opened the wine, one tried to unsquash the baguettes from where he had fallen on them earlier. Patrick, however brought out the coup de grace. Amazing food flowed from his rucksack like manna from heaven. There was foie gras with truffles, pain bagnat, with glorious tomato juices running down the side, and hot pumpkin and fontina cheese soup. The best of all, however, was a glass jar of this chicken, all lemon-yellow and oily and amazingly juicy, which was ladled into baguettes with crisp lettuce and mayonnaise – unforgettable.

Serves 6

Preparation: 20 minutes, plus 12 hours' marinating

Cooking: 15 minutes

6 free-range chicken breasts

1 litre/1¾ pints hot Chicken Stock (see page 187)

zest and juice of 2 lemons

1 garlic clove

200 ml/7 fl oz extra-virgin olive oil (the yellowy French oils are best for this)

8 thyme sprigs

salt and pepper

Poach the whole chicken breasts in the hot stock for 10 minutes, until just cooked. Remove and allow to cool while you prepare the marinade.

Peel the zest off the lemons with a potato peeler and place in a bowl with the lemon juice. Slice the garlic clove into thin slices and add to the lemon. Pour in all the olive oil and mix well. Rub the thyme between your hands to release the oils and add to the bowl. Season the mixture well.

Slice the breasts, which should still be warm and juicy, crossways into 6 pieces each. Pour the marinade over the chicken and season well. Pour the lot into a kilner (preserving) jar and leave in the fridge for 12 hours before eating. It is brilliant in sandwiches or with rocket as a classy summer salad. It will keep in the fridge for a week.

Confit of goose or duck

Confit is goose or duck, slowly cooked and then preserved in the fat. Obviously this dish will not appeal to you if you lie in bed at night thinking about the state of your heart. However, don't worry. First, the pleasure you get from eating confit is much greater than any possible health problems that may arise and second, most of the fat drains off when you roast it at the end. Make sure you make lots as it keeps for at least 3 months.

Serves 2
Preparation: 5 minutes
Cooking: 2–3 hours

2 goose legs (or duck legs)
salt and pepper
500 ml/17 fl oz goose or duck fat
1 thyme sprig, crumbled
1 garlic clove, chopped

Start by rubbing the goose or duck legs with salt and pepper. Heat the goose or duck fat in a casserole and lay the legs in it, making sure they are covered by fat. Sprinkle over the thyme and garlic. Place in a medium (150°C/300°F/Gas Mark 2) oven for 2 hours or until the legs are tender to the tip of a knife – the flesh should be willing to pull away from the bone.

Now you can either pack the legs in their fat in a kilner (preserving) jar for storage, or place them in a really hot oven (230°C/450°F/Gas Mark 8) for 15 minutes to crisp up. Serve one leg per person with redcurrant jelly and a peppery salad dressed with balsamic vinegar.

Chicken pot-roasted in thyme and hay

This is a cracking technique for cooking perfectly juicy meat, with a real country taste. The hay and thyme soak up some of the liquid and keep the meat incredibly moist, as well as imparting a delicate hint of flavour. Make sure you use good dry hay for this – hay from upland pastures is best as it brings the aroma of wild flowers and herbs. The basic method of sealing in the meat with paste and enfolding it in steamy hay works for all sorts of dishes – try searing a rack of lamb and cooking it for 15 minutes – the results are pretty impressive.

Serves 4
Preparation: 10 minutes
Cooking: 1½ hours

1 large bunch of thyme

a double handful of hay
(you can use hay from a pet shop)

3 garlic cloves, unpeeled

1 free-range chicken or guinea fowl, about 1–1.5 kg/2–3 lb

25 g/1 oz butter

1 tsp sea salt

1 glass white wine

Flour paste (this glues on the casserole lid – it is not meant to be eaten and tastes pretty awful):

250 g/8 oz plain flour

1 tbsp salt

cold water

Dig out your biggest cast-iron casserole dish or terracotta pot with a good lid. The bird should fit in with room to spare. Now mix the thyme with the hay and lay one-third of it on the bottom of the casserole. Smash the garlic and throw it in among the hay. Nestle the chicken or guinea fowl in the hay. Rub the butter over the chicken, sprinkle with salt, then pour over the wine. Pile the rest of the hay around the bird.

Preheat the oven to 220°C/425°F/Gas Mark 7. Now make the flour paste seal. Mix just enough water with the flour and salt to make a firm elastic dough. Roll this out into a long sausage and stick it all the way around the rim of the casserole. Press the lid on firmly and make sure an air-tight seal is achieved. Place in the hot oven for 80–90 minutes.

Remove and cut open the lid to reveal a beautifully cooked chicken, moist and yummy, redolent of garlic, thyme and the countryside. Carve the chicken and pour over the juices from the bottom of the pan.

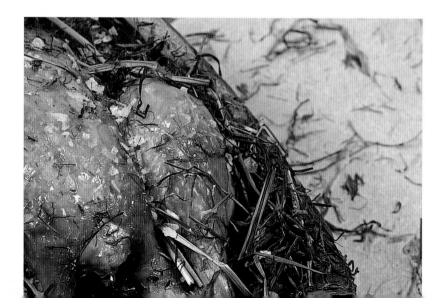

Chicken thighs stuffed with gremolata in a rich tomato sauce

This is a recipe I have cooked for many years, always with great success. The lemony gremolata stuffing is a heaven-sent partner for the chicken. Always use thighs, as they have a firmer texture and much more flavour than breasts. Also, don't stint on the olive oil, the sauce needs to be rich and and you want to see the gorgeous golden oil seeping out of it.

Serves 4 for as a main course, 8 as a starter
Preparation: 45 minutes, plus resting
Cooking: 30 minutes

Gremolata:

zest and juice of 2 unwaxed lemons

2 garlic cloves, finely chopped

large handful of fresh brown breadcrumbs

large bunch of flat-leaf parsley, coarsely chopped

1 small red onion, finely chopped

1 tbsp capers

4 tbsp olive oil

salt and pepper

12 slices Parma or Bayonne ham

8 chicken thighs, boned and skinned

olive oil, for cooking

Sauce:

3 good glugs of olive oil

1 red onion, chopped

1 sweet red romano pepper, deseeded and chopped

300 g/10 oz ripe cherry tomatoes, halved

1 garlic clove, chopped

3 anchovies

1 tbsp capers

1 tbsp chopped basil

1 tbsp chopped oregano

½ glass white wine

salt and pepper

First, make the gremolata. In a bowl, mix the lemon juice and zest with the garlic, breadcrumbs, parsley, onion, capers and olive oil. Season well and let the mixture rest for 10 minutes.

Now lay 8 slices of ham on a board. Place a thigh on top of each ham slice and put a spoonful of gremolata on top. Roll up into 8 parcels. Cut the remaining 4 pieces of ham in half lengthways and roll them around each of the parcels to cover the open ends. To hold everything in place, push a bamboo skewer through each. These parcels can be made some time in advance and kept in the fridge. To cook, sauté in olive oil for 10 minutes each side, then finish under the grill for a few minutes.

For the sauce, heat the olive oil in a heavy pan, and add the onion, pepper, tomatoes, garlic, anchovies and capers. Simmer over a medium heat until the tomatoes start to break up. Throw in the herbs and the wine (use the wine that you are going to drink with the finished dish). Season the sauce and break down any still-firm tomatoes with a fork.

Serve 1 thigh for a starter, or 2 for a main course. Ladle the sauce into the centre of a plate and slice the chicken thighs into two.

Lemon and tarragon griddled chicken thighs

Tarragon is the daddy of all herbs in my book. There are very few herbs with this intensity of flavour, and as a result there are a limited number of things it complements, but chicken is definitely one of them. I like to use leg quarters which have had the thigh part boned out, then griddle or barbecue them.

Serves 4

Preparation: 5 minutes, plus at least 2 hours' marinating

Cooking: 15 minutes

4 chicken leg quarters

6 tarragon sprigs

zest and juice of 1 lemon

1 tbsp cider vinegar

2 garlic cloves, mashed

good grinding of black pepper

pinch of cayenne

50 ml/2 fl oz olive oil

First things first – debone the chicken thighs. Don't be daunted, this is really easy to do. Lay the leg quarter skin-side down on a chopping board and run a small sharp knife along both sides of the thigh bone. When you have released the bone from the thigh meat, cut through the joint between the drumstick and the thigh. This should leave you with the whole leg with no bone in the thigh. Thus everything cooks evenly and the drumstick gives the eater something to hang on to.

Now chop up the tarragon coarsely and put in a mixing bowl. Add all the other ingredients and mix well. Marinate the chicken for at least 2 hours. Brush off the bulk of the marinade and cook on a medium-hot griddle or barbecue for 7–8 minutes on each side. Pour some of the marinade over the chicken as it cooks if you don't mind smoke.

Serve the legs with a green herb salad and duck-fat chips or sauté potatoes.

Baby chickens, North-African style

Although I am straying south a little with this dish, it is really easy and foolproof, even for those of you who don't cook very often. North Africa, and Morocco in particular, has had a strong influence on me ever since I travelled through southern France, where this style of cooking is popular. You just can't beat the characteristic mixture of pungent capers, fruity olive oil, chilli and tomato.

Serves 4
Preparation: 10 minutes
Cooking: 1 hour

4 poussins (baby chickens)

100 ml/3½ fl oz olive oil

4 garlic cloves, crushed

2 red onions, sliced

2 red chillies, deseeded and sliced in 4 lengthwise

200 g/7 oz green olives

100 g/3½ oz capers (rinse if very salty)

2 x 400 g/13 oz cans chopped tomatoes

1 glass white wine

12 mint leaves

small bunch fresh coriander (stalks and leaves)

If you wish, tie together the legs of the poussins with string. Pour all the olive oil into a large casserole. Heat up, then add the crushed garlic. Let the garlic sizzle for 1 minute, then brown the poussins, breast-sides down. When they have taken on a good colour, after about 5 minutes, remove them, and add the onions to the pan.

Allow the onions to soften in the olive oil for a few minutes, then start adding the rest of the ingredients. First the chillies, then the olives and capers, and finally the tomatoes. Now add the wine and give the mixture a good stir.

Nestle the browned poussins in the sauce, and put the lid on the casserole. Either cook on the hob for 45 minutes over a low heat, or put the pot in the oven for 45 minutes at 180°C/350°F/Gas Mark 4. Check the poussins by inserting a knife in the thighs – the juices should run clear. Serve them with couscous or flat bread, and sprinkle on the mint leaves and coriander.

Hot-smoked honeyed duck breasts

If you have a box smoker (available from good kitchen shops), this is too easy for words, and provides you with the basis for all sorts of summery salads and cold dishes. I like to serve the duck breasts sliced thinly with rocket and Roasted Rosemary Tomatoes (see page 152). I prefer cherry wood for smoking, but commercial oakwood chippings work fine.

Serves 4

Preparation: 15 minutes, plus 4 hours' marinating

Cooking: 15 minutes

1 tbsp honey
1 tbsp chopped thyme
1 tbsp strong old balsamic vinegar
pinch of allspice
salt and pepper
4 duck breasts

Mix the marinade ingredients together in a bowl and rub the mix well into the breasts. I like to score the fat on the breasts lightly in a criss-cross fashion to allow the marinade to penetrate. Leave to marinate for 4 hours or so in the fridge.

Put 2 handfuls of chippings in the bottom of the smoker, and put the breasts in. Place the smoker over a medium gas flame for 15 minutes. This will cook them pink. Allow them to cool, then serve however you like. They will keep for a week in the fridge.

Sautéed guinea fowl with a white-wine sauce

At 21 I entered my first professional kitchen. The restaurant was a tiny 30-seat place in the French Alps. The owner/chef/barman was called Michel and he had somewhat nervously agreed to take me on in the role of Plongeur (dishwasher and general slave). Michel is from Normandy, home of apples, cream, and cider, and cooks in the traditional way. That is, he tries to give as many of his customers high blood pressure and heart attacks as possible. The risk of these ailments is negated, however, by regular small doses of red wine, cider and calvados. The kitchen was of course tiny, but always spotless, and had a particular aroma of rich cream sauces and aniseed. This recipe was (and may still be) one of his favourites and the first I learned to cook. I love it to this day.

Serves 4
Preparation: 15 minutes
Cooking: 25 minutes

4 guinea fowl breasts
50 ml/2 fl oz olive oil
1 tbsp chopped thyme
2 tbsp wholegrain mustard
salt and freshly ground pepper
3 knobs of butter
2 shallots, finely chopped
1 garlic clove, chopped
100 ml/3½ fl oz white wine or cider
50 ml/2 fl oz double cream
12 slices eating apple, peeled
1 tbsp honey

Cut slashes in the guinea fowl breasts and rub them with olive oil, some of the fresh thyme, mustard and salt and freshly ground pepper. Heat a knob of butter in a heavy-based frying pan until it foams. Add the guinea fowl and sauté for 10 minutes on each side. Remove the guinea fowl and keep warm.

In the same pan, heat another knob of butter and add the shallots, garlic and remaining thyme and fry, stirring, until the shallot is softened, around 2–3 minutes. Pour in the white wine or cider, bring to the boil and cook briskly until reduced (about 10 minutes), then add the double cream. Cook over a high heat until reduced to a thick consistency and a rich, golden colour.

Meanwhile, heat the third knob of butter in a heavy-based frying pan. Add the apple slices and honey and fry until the apple is caramelised. Spoon the cream sauce onto a warm serving plate. Slice the guinea fowl breasts and place on top of the sauce. Garnish with the caramelised apple and serve at once.

Stuffed poussins baked in the coals

This is a wonderful recipe to cook on the barbecue or any open fire. If you haven't got a fire, then roast them in the oven at the hottest possible setting. The smells and juices when you rip open the foil are amazing. All you need to have with this are sauté potatoes and bread and I would drink a really cold crisp rosé.

Serves 4
Preparation: 20 minutes
Cooking: 45 minutes

1 tbsp olive oil

2 garlic cloves, chopped

2 celery sticks, sliced

2 onions, chopped

2 carrots, chopped

small bunch of thyme, leaves stripped off

100 g/3½ oz pancetta fat or Lardo (cured pork fat from Italy, available from good delis)

4 chicken livers

1 glass of white wine

4 poussins

olive oil, for rubbing

salt and pepper

parsley, to scatter

large needle and cotton thread, for stitching

20 x 25 cm/10 in square pieces of foil

Heat the olive oil in a pan and add the chopped garlic, celery, onions and carrot. Add half the thyme. Sweat the vegetables until they are soft, about 10 minutes.

Now chop up the fat or Lardo, and the chicken livers. Add to the vegetables and mix with the wine. Stuff the mixture into each poussin: they should all be pretty full. Stitch up the opening in the poussins, and rub them with oil, and salt and pepper. Sprinkle the poussins with the rest of the thyme, and wrap each one in 5 layers of foil.

Let the fire or barbecue burn down to embers, and bury the poussins for 45 minutes. Remove them with tongs and blow off the ash. If you are using the oven, preheat it to its hottest setting, and cook for 45 minutes.

Snip the foil open carefully and pour any juices into a bowl. Cut each poussin in half with shears, and scoop out the stuffing. Serve the poussins on top of the stuffing, and pour over the juices. Fantastic!

salads

introduction

What is a salad? This is a tricky one. I suppose that when I think of a salad, the first thing that comes to mind is a big bowl of crisp green leaves, mixed up with lovely fresh herbs, all coated with the thinnest layer possible of oily dressing. For the last two years I have developed a real interest in growing salads (advancing years!) and now revel in rows of mixed leaves and rocket every summer. These types of leaves are so easy to grow, you just have to throw the seeds in a scrape in the ground and three weeks later the leaves appear. For me, nothing beats the gentle pleasure of going down to the garden (or window box) and cutting the rocket just before lunch or dinner, and no shop-bought leaves match the flavour. I also love not having to pay supermarket prices for a mere six leaves.

I think the whole point of a salad is that it should encompass a spectrum of textures: warm bubbling cheese, silky Parma ham and crunchy, oily croûtons dripping with earthy flavour. All that combined with a sharp mustardy dressing and the crunchy salad leaves ensure a perfect lunch.

If we are pushing the boundaries a bit, I see no reason why a plate of lightly sautéed wild mushrooms, tossed with rocket and dressing, then laid on a bed of jambon cru or prosciutto, should not be called a salad. This works if I use the definition given by my chum Joe Wadsack, wine expert extraordinaire: a salad is anything cold you would eat outdoors, with a glass of cold rosé on a hot summer's day. By this definition, salads have endless possibilities and come in all guises, from warm salads of potato and onion, all dripping in mustardy vinaigrette, to the finest of leaves in a bowl.

Fennel salad

I love the aniseed crunch of fennel, which goes perfectly with anything oily and fishy.

Serves 4
Preparation: 5 minutes

2 bulbs of fennel
small bunch of fennel herb, finely chopped
50 g/2 oz watercress
1 lemon
2 tbsp fruity olive oil
salt and pepper

Slice the fennel wafer-thin, either with a knife or a mandolin. Place the fennel, fennel herb, watercress, lemon juice and half the olive oil in a bag, and shake gently. Leave in the bag for 5 minutes, then pile on a plate. To finish off, zest the lemon over the salad, and dribble the rest of the oil around.

Warm potato, lemon and olive oil salad

What can beat a good hearty potato salad, especially when there is some really well-flavoured olive oil to hand. The key is to assemble this salad when the potatoes are warm, but not hot; about 10 minutes after you have cooked and drained them is fine.

Serves 4
Preparation: 5 minutes
Cooking: 20 minutes

zest and juice of 1 unwaxed lemon
50 ml/2 fl oz good fruity olive oil
12 mint leaves
sea salt and pepper
625 g/1¼ lb new potatoes, cooked until just tender

Put the zest and juice of the lemon into a bowl. Add the olive oil, and chop up the mint leaves. Mix everything together gently with a fork, and taste for seasoning. If the potatoes are large, cut them in half; if small, leave them whole, and add them to the dressing. Leave the salad to rest for 2–3 minutes, then serve. This would go down a treat with a rib of rare Angus beef.

Salad Lyonnais

I don't know exactly why, but when it comes to salads I always come back to France. This particular salad is one I had in a village called Biot near Nice. It was in one of those restaurants where the waitress writes your order on a corner of a tablecloth then tears it off to take to the kitchen. The salad came on big earthenware plates with the herrings in a huge bowl on the side.

Serves 4

Preparation time: 10 minutes

300 g/10 oz new potatoes (I like to use the waxy Ratte variety)

2 free-range eggs

8 marinated herring fillets (you can buy these in any supermarket)

2 tbsp flat-leaf parsley

1 frisée lettuce, washed and roughly torn up.

1 large shallot, finely sliced

1 tbsp capers

Dressing:

1 tbsp Dijon mustard

1 tbsp red wine vinegar

4 tbsp best olive oil

1 tsp marinating liquid from the fish

salt and pepper

First, boil the potatoes. Give them about 10 minutes until they are just cooked. While they are on, boil the eggs for 7 minutes – you want firm whites and a hint of runniness in the yolks (only use the very best free-range eggs in this dish).

Slice the herrings into strips and chop up the parsley. Finally, make the dressing by whisking all the ingredients together and adding a little salt and pepper to taste.

To assemble the salad, put a pile of frisée leaves into each bowl and place some strips of herring on top. Thickly slice the potatoes and roughly scatter them over, followed by some egg quarters, parsley and sliced shallot and some herbs. Now give each bowl a few capers for luck, then pour on the dressing.

Your guests should give their salads a bit of a mix at the table to make sure the dressing coats all the different ingredients, then tuck in. This should be accompanied by bread and cold white wine.

Perfect green salad

A green salad is a glorious thing when done properly, and the perfect accompaniment to steaks, cold roast beef or anything cheesy. But what exactly is it? The French would say that a green salad is a bowl of beautifully crisp leaves, all of the same variety, and with a good dressing. While that's great, I prefer a bit of variation, with a seasonal selection of salad leaves, as well as some leafy green herbs.

'A dressing is not a compote, a dressing is not a custard, a dressing is oil, vinegar, salt, pepper and mustard.' So said the poet Ogden Nash, and he was dead right. A salad like this deserves something simple, so follow the poem and you will not go far wrong. One tip: use about three parts oil to one part vinegar.

Serves 6
Preparation: 5 minutes

1 frisée lettuce
1 little gem lettuce
1 lollo rosso
small bunch of flat-leaf parsley
handful of baby spinach
8 mint leaves
dressing, to serve

Rip handfuls of frisée off the lettuce, and wash well, together with the little gem and lollo rosso (I only use the inner leaves of the lollo rosso, since the outer ones can be a little floppy). It is a good idea to wash the leaves in a sink full of cold water to which you have added a handful of salt. This will make the leaves extra crispy, and make any unwanted protein drop to the bottom. Spin the leaves to remove the water, tear them up a little and throw them in a bowl. Pull the parsley leaves off the stalks, leaving them whole, and throw them in too. Now add the whole spinach leaves and the mint. Toss well and add a few drops of dressing, then toss again and serve.

Scallop, smoked salmon and watercress salad

This is a terribly decadent salad that obviously does not get made all that often. Having said that, it works wonderfully well and is something of a favourite. I make it when I get hold of some of my favourite Frøya scallops. The scallops are at their best 'cooked' in the dressing, with no heat involved.

Serves 4

Preparation: 10 minutes, plus marinating

Dressing:

2 tbsp extra-virgin olive oil

1 shallot, finely chopped

½ garlic clove, finely chopped

1 tbsp finely chopped mint, to taste

juice of 2 lemons

dash of white wine vinegar

salt and freshly ground black pepper

4 good-quality scallops, raw but shelled

a handful of rocket leaves

a handful of watercress sprigs

200 g/7 oz smoked wild salmon, thickly sliced

flat-leaf parsley, finely chopped, to garnish

First make the dressing. Mix together the olive oil, shallot, garlic, mint, lemon juice and the white wine vinegar, and season with salt and freshly ground black pepper.

Slice the scallops into discs. Toss the sliced scallops with half the dressing (reserving the remaining dressing). Marinate the scallops in the refrigerator for at least 1 hour.

Pile the rocket and watercress on a serving plate and arrange the marinated scallops in the centre. Arrange the smoked wild salmon around the scallops. Drizzle the remaining dressing over the salad, sprinkle with parsley and serve with lovely warm brown bread and salty Normandy butter.

Shepherd's salad

This defines the hearty style of French main-course salad. To the French, a salad can be all sorts of things: from a few leaves with a drizzle of good oil to a salad like this one – a real mountain meal on a plate that a lumberjack or shepherd wouldn't be embarrassed to eat in front of women.

I ate this for the first time in a tiny auberge in the Alps where the food is unbelievable and also amazing value. I hope I can do this salad justice.

Serves 4
Preparation: 30 minutes
Cooking: 15 minutes

Dressing:

2 tbsp wholegrain mustard

juice of ½ lemon

splash of cider vinegar

100 ml/3½ fl oz sunflower oil

1 tbsp honey

salt and pepper

8 slices French loaf, cut into small chunks for croûtons

1 tbsp olive oil

1 Chevrotin, or small goat's cheese (use any creamy goat's cheese, not the crumbly stuff)

bowlful of mixed, washed leaves: frisée, lollo rosso, and little gem

3 tbsp dressing

100 g/3½ oz cornichons (baby gherkins)

100 g/3½ oz white cocktail onions in vinegar

2 tbsp capers

8 good large, thin slices of air-dried ham: San Daniele, Bayonne or Serrano are all acceptable

16 slices saucisson sec or other air-dried sausage

400 g/13 oz new potatoes, boiled and left warm

First make the dressing: mix all the ingredients together with a whisk until the dressing is thick. To make the croûtons, toss the chunks of bread in olive oil in a heavy pan over a medium heat until they are crisp and golden. Please don't cook them in the oven as this dries them out. A croûton should be crispy crunchy on the outside and chewy in the middle.

Now, preheat the grill and cut the goat's cheese into 5 mm/¼ inch cubes. Place these under the grill on a baking sheet to cook until just golden.

Meanwhile, toss the salad leaves in the dressing and pile into big shallow bowls. Sprinkle randomly with cornichons and onions, and a few capers. Tear up the ham and throw it onto the salad, then do the same with the sausage. Don't cover the lettuce with meat – a balance is what's needed. Cut the warm potatoes into smallish pieces and sprinkle over. All the time try to keep some height in the salad, so that the ingredients don't squish the lettuce.

Finally, sprinkle the croûtons over and, using a spatula, flick small melted chunks of cheese randomly over the salad. Serve the remaining dressing on the side with good bread and some pungent red wine.

Wild wood mushrooms with air-dried ham

A lot of people would say that this is not a salad at all. After all, it is a plate of ham and mushrooms, right? But I think it is definitely a salad, just not in the conventional sense. Accompany it with lots of really good bread, as well as some cold white Burgundy. If you intend to collect wild mushrooms yourself, always take a good guide book with you, to identify the edible varieties. If in doubt, leave out!

Serves 2
Preparation: 10 minutes
Cooking: 10 minutes

Salad:

200 g/7 oz wild mushrooms, ideally mixed ceps and chanterelles

2 tbsp olive oil

12 slices of air-dried ham, such as prosciutto, Parma ham or Bayonne ham

a double handful of peppery young rocket leaves

Parmesan cheese, for shavings

salt and pepper

Dressing:

juice of 1 lemon

2 tbsp olive oil

1 tbsp good balsamic vinegar

salt and black pepper

First, trim the base of the ceps with a sharp knife to remove any woody or dirty bits. Now slice the ceps lengthways into 4 slices. Leave any chanterelles whole, but brush off the dirt carefully. Do not wash the mushrooms – they soak up water like a sponge and this will ruin the dish. In a hot pan, sauté the mushrooms in olive oil until just tender. Season and remove from the pan.

Mix the dressing ingredients in a bowl and season. Now mix the ham with the rocket in a random but artistic fashion, and spread on a platter, ideally a rustic wooden one. Make a well in the salad and pile the mushrooms in the middle. Spoon the dressing all over and sprinkle with shavings of nutty Parmesan.

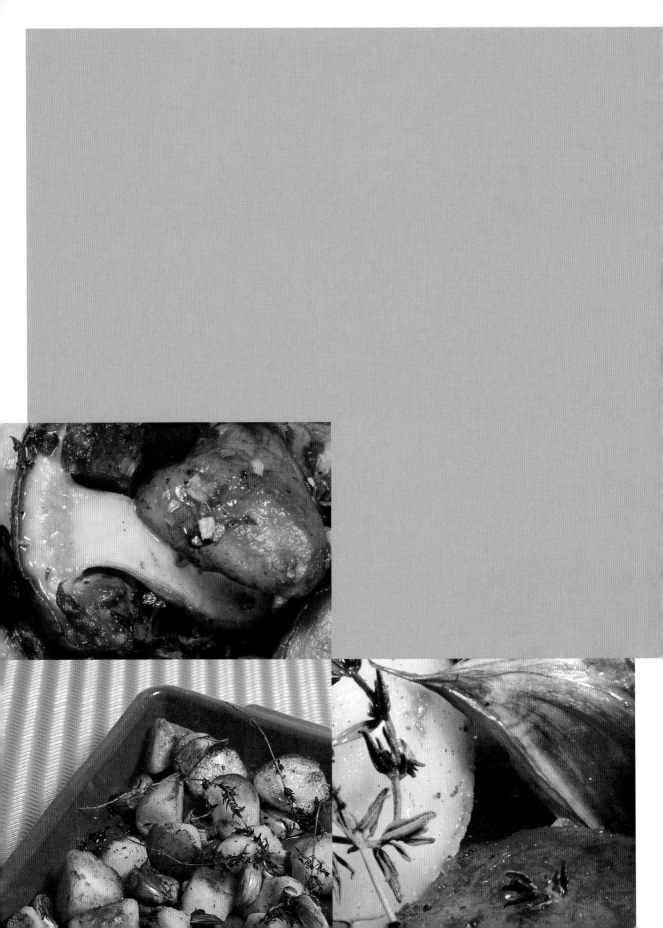

vegetables

introduction

Although this is the Vegetables chapter, I am sure some of you will be quick to point out that this section is not necessarily vegetarian. It is about dishes that predominantly contain vegetables, but may require a little smoked pancetta to give them that final touch of perfection. That said, when I sat down to write this book I found to my surprise that I had more ideas for mainly veggie recipes than any others. A lot of this is due to Italian influence. My friend Gennaro has made me look at vegetables in a new and simple light, where the less you do to a thing, the better it tastes.

The advent and growing popularity of organic farming have made a huge difference to the quality of the veg we eat. People say that they are put off by the cost of organic goods, but to my mind it really is worth paying the difference.

Boulangère potatoes

This is just about the most versatile potato dish there is – it's much lighter than its cousin, Dauphinoise potatoes, and thus more suitable to accompanying a wide range of dishes. In the old days in France, people would bring their potatoes to the village baker at the end of the day's baking to slowly cook in the dying heat of the wood oven. To stop them drying out, they would cover them in stock and add sliced onions. The next morning, they would collect the cooked potatoes, which would have absorbed most of the stock and the flavour from the onions.

Serves 6
Preparation: 20 minutes
Cooking: 1 hour

25 g/1 oz butter

2 large onions, sliced

2 garlic cloves, chopped

1 kg/2 lb of baking potatoes, peeled and sliced

300 ml/½ pint Chicken Stock (see page 187)

150 ml/¼ pint white wine

1 tbsp chopped thyme and/or 1 tbsp rosemary

salt and pepper

Preheat the oven to 180°C/350°F/Gas Mark 4. Melt the butter in a heavy pan and cook the onions until they are soft and translucent. Add the chopped garlic and sweat for a minute. Add the potatoes, salt, pepper, and the liquid ingredients. Mix well and pour into a baking dish. Bake in the oven for 1 hour.

Check occasionally that the potatoes are not burning. If it looks like they are, cover the dish with foil for the rest of the cooking time. They should be golden, soft and aromatic, and most of the liquid should have been absorbed. Sprinkle with the chopped herbs before serving.

Dauphinoise potatoes

Dauphinoise potato is rich beyond compare, causes cardiologists and dieticians to despair, and is without a doubt every foodie's favourite potato dish. There are also more recipes for it than there are Japanese cars. So why does everyone have problems with it? In recent years chefs have tried to make the dish lighter and less heart-attack inducing. To my mind this defeats the object – surely it is better to eat the original occasionally, rather than the insipid half-hearted thing that is passed off as Dauphinoise, regularly. Many people complain that it splits in the oven, or never comes together into a creamy mass – the simple reason is that the fat content is not high enough. Proper Dauphinoise contains potatoes, garlic, seasoning, and DOUBLE cream. Nothing else. No low-fat cream and skimmed or semi-skimmed milk, no wine and no cheese. I promise that if you follow this recipe, it will work. You may have to experiment a little with timing, because no two ovens cook exactly the same, but it will work. If you want to sprinkle a handful of grated Gruyère cheese over the top 10 minutes before the end of cooking, the bistro gods will forgive you!

Serves 6

Preparation: 15 minutes

Cooking: 55 minutes

1 kg/2 lb baking potatoes, peeled and fairly finely sliced (Russets or King Edwards are good)

salt and pepper

2 garlic cloves, finely chopped

400 ml/14 fl oz double cream or full-fat crème fraîche

If you have one, use a good ceramic or terracotta baking dish. Preheat the oven to 160°C/325°F/Gas Mark 3. In a mixing bowl, season the sliced potatoes well and mix with the garlic. Add the cream and mix well. Now pour out the mix into your dish – it should come to just below the top – and check that the cream comes to just below the top layer of potato. Pat the potato down with the back of a spoon so it forms a solid layer. Bake in the oven for 40 minutes, then check it. If the cream looks like it is splitting, your oven is too hot, so turn it down by 10°C/25°F/1 Gas Mark. Bake for another 15 minutes, then remove. The gratin should be golden on top and the potato well-cooked. The slices of potato will have cooked down to a perfectly creamy, quite solid mass that just oozes garlic.

Serve with anything you like, but I love this with pink, juicy, tender lamb, or a blackened steak, running with carmine juices that mingle with the garlicky potato.

Goose-fat roast potatoes
with thyme and garlic

Goose and duck fat are fabulous substances. People think of them as unhealthy, but if you look at the Perigord region of France, where these fats are an everyday part of the diet, along with red wine and Gauloises, it is interesting that people live longer there than in any other part of the country. What is important to us, though, is that they flavour roast potatoes like nothing else on earth. Combine them with garlic and thyme, and I need say no more.

Serves 6
Preparation: 15 minutes
Cooking: 47 minutes

12 floury potatoes, peeled and halved
4 tbsp goose or duck fat
a good bunch of thyme
12 whole garlic cloves, unpeeled
sea salt and black pepper

First parboil the potatoes for 7 minutes. Drain them then take them outside and shake the pan vigorously. The cold air does something amazing – all the water evaporates in a flash, and the edges of the potato fluff up beautifully.

Preheat the oven to 200°C/400°F/Gas Mark 6. Now take a heavy cast-iron skillet, or a really heavy roasting dish and put it on the highest heat on the hob that you can. Spoon the fat into the pan and wait until it gets really hot. Now add the potatoes and let them colour up really well for 10 minutes.

Just before you put the pan in the oven, scatter the thyme, stalks and all, in with the potatoes. Bash each garlic clove with the heel of your hand and add them too (don't skin the garlic or it will burn) then mix everything well. Make sure the potatoes are well coated with fat. Sprinkle with sea salt and black pepper and cook in the oven for 30 minutes or so. Serve with rare roast beef and Yorkshire puddings also cooked in duck fat and everyone will treat you like Wellington after Waterloo (unless they are French, of course).

Rosti

Aside from fondue, I think rosti is the one uniquely Swiss addition to the world's culinary heritage. I have seen many recipes for rosti over the years, and I am always amazed by how many ingredients some chefs try to put in. A rosti should be a simply glorious golden and crunchy grated potato cake. That's it. Having said that, a lot of people have problems getting them to work. I promise that this recipe solves all those problems.

Serves 4
Preparation: 10 minutes
Cooking: 10–15 minutes

2 large potatoes (King Edward)
salt and pepper
50 g/2 oz melted butter

Peel the potatoes and grate them coarsely. Now take a clean tea towel and squeeze the grated potatoes for all you are worth. This is crucial: rosti will not work if you leave all the water in. Now place the potatoes in a bowl and season well. Pour the melted butter into the potato and stir it in.

Heat a dry non-stick pan until medium hot. Drop in dollops of potato. Press out the rosti with the back of a spoon and leave to cook for 5 minutes. Try to resist messing around with them too much, as they are prone to breaking up in the early stages. Turn the cakes over and cook for 5 minutes more. They should be golden, crunchy and delicious. You can cook these in advance and warm them up in the oven when you need them. A rosti with a fried egg on top and some crispy bacon is my idea of breakfast heaven.

Alpine potato and prune cake

Farcement savoyarde, to give it its proper name, is a French Alpine speciality. This amazing potato and prune recipe is totally unbelievable to eat, especially with a good hearty stew, or a piece of roasted chicken.

Serves 6

Preparation: 20 minutes

Cooking: 3 hours

3 onions, peeled and sliced

knob of butter

2 garlic cloves, chopped

1 kg/2 lb potato, peeled and grated

2 eggs

200 ml/7 fl oz crème fraîche or double cream

300 g/10 oz prunes, pitted and chopped

24 slices streaky bacon

Soften the onions in the butter for a few minutes in a hot pan. Add the garlic, sweat for 1 minute, then take off the heat. In a big mixing bowl, mix the grated potatoes with the onion and garlic, and add the eggs. Stir in the crème fraîche and prunes and season well. The mixture should not be too sloppy, so add the cream bit by bit. Pretty soon you will judge by eye how to get it just right.

Butter a pudding basin and line it with bacon slices, making sure the bottom and sides are covered and that the bacon overhangs the sides. Now pour in the mixture, to within an inch of the top and fold over the overhanging bacon. Put a saucer or something similar on top of the mix and sit the basin in a big saucepan with a couple of fingers of water in it. Put a lid on the saucepan and place over a very low heat. Steam for 3 hours, checking occasionally that the pan has not boiled dry.

Turn the cake out onto a plate and slice. Serve with stew or roast chicken. It is brilliant with Boeuf Bourgignon, something to do with the combination of prunes and beef, I think.

Bubble and squeak

Bubble and squeak is one of Britain's great inventions – a typical leftovers dish. Traditionally very rustic and covered in crunchy burnt bits, it has now become trendy and is to be found in all the best places, as an accompaniment to any rich stew. My grandmother always used to say it was called bubble and squeak because of the chemical effect on one's innards. My father would agree, but then he always blames the poor dog anyway.

Serves 4–6

Preparation: 10 minutes

Cooking: 40 minutes

1/4 Savoy cabbage, finely sliced

1 onion, sliced

25 g/1 oz butter

500 g/1 lb dry mashed potato

200 g/7 oz peas

oil, for frying (use duck fat or lard if the state of your heart is no cause for concern)

salt and pepper

Boil the cabbage and onion in salted water for 20 minutes, then drain and cool. Work the butter into the potato, making sure it stays fairly dry in texture. Now mix in the cabbage, onion and peas and season well. Form the bubble into cakes and fry in oil or fat for 10 minutes on each side. The outside should be beautifully golden and the cakes should stay firm.

Tartiflette

This is one of my top three desert-island recipes. There are many different variations on the same theme, but I believe this one to be without peer. It is originally the recipe of my chum André Corneloup, who runs the café that, in my opinion, serves the best mountain food in France.

Serves 4
Preparation: 30 minutes
Cooking: 45 minutes

8 potatoes, peeled and sliced

50 g/2 oz butter

1 tbsp olive oil

2 large onions, sliced

4 garlic cloves, peeled and sliced

200 g/ 7 oz smoked bacon lardons (try to get French poitrine fumé, or failing that Italian pancetta)

4 thyme sprigs

1 glass white wine

100 ml/3½ fl oz double or single cream

salt and freshly ground black pepper

500 g/1 lb Reblochon cheese (no other cheese will do!)

Parboil the sliced potatoes for 5 minutes until they just start to soften. At this point drain and dry them. In a big, heavy pan melt the butter and oil together and add the sliced onions and garlic. Cook over a strong heat until they start to colour. Throw in the lardons and cook for 5 minutes. Now add the potatoes, and turn down the heat. I like to let the mixture cook slowly for a good 15 minutes, before the next stage.

Preheat the oven to 220°C/425°F/Gas Mark 7. Now add the thyme, white wine and cream to the pan, and let it all warm through for a minute. Season the mixture well at this point, but remember that the bacon is salty. Tip the mixture into a baking dish, and cover with strips of Reblochon. Cook in a hot oven for 20 minutes. When it is done, the cheese should have melted into the potatoes and onions leaving a golden crust on top. Like so many cheesy recipes, this only needs a salad and some crisp white wine to accompany it.

A word of warning: do not drink water with this, as it will turn the cheese to lead inside you. At the end of the meal I really recommend a glass or two of Poire William, which seems to settle things down.

Green beans with tomatoes and garlic

In this great little recipe, the beans are not boiled, but roasted in olive oil and white wine. The result is brilliant: the beans stay firm, and go really well with any simple roast.

Serves 4
Preparation: 20 minutes
Cooking: 20 minutes

450 g/14½ oz green beans, topped and tailed

150 g/5 oz cherry tomatoes, quartered

4 garlic cloves, peeled and coarsely chopped

4 tbsp olive oil

1 glass white wine

salt and pepper

zest and juice of 1 lemon

a handful of chopped flat-leaf parsley

Preheat the oven to 200°C/400°F/Gas Mark 6. In a baking dish, mix the beans, cherry tomatoes, garlic, and olive oil. Add half of the white wine, the lemon zest and juice, and season well. Cover the dish with foil, and place in a hot oven.

After 10 minutes, remove, stir well and add the rest of the wine. This time, leave the foil off and cook for a further 10 minutes at the same temperature, then remove and add the parsley. The tomatoes will have broken down, leaving the beans coated with oily, tomatoey goo.

Roasted rosemary tomatoes

These are so easy and there are so few ingredients involved that I was a bit embarrassed about including them. They are so good, however, that I do them pretty much every week at home.

Serves 6

Preparation: 6 minutes

Cooking: 20–30 minutes

6 bunches of cherry tomatoes, on the vine, about 750 g/ 1½ lb

6 tbsp olive oil

18 garlic cloves, unpeeled and lightly squashed

6 rosemary sprigs

sea salt

juice of ½ lemon

Preheat the oven to 200°C/400°F/Gas Mark 6. In a big bowl, mix the cherry tomatoes (still on the vine), olive oil and most of the garlic. Break the rosemary into manageable-sized pieces and mix it in gently. Pour out onto an oven tray or a terracotta oven dish and sprinkle with salt. Roast in the oven for 20 minutes or until the tomatoes are starting to pop, but still hold their shape. Remove from the oven, and sprinkle the lemon juice over. Throw in a few pieces of the reserved garlic before serving.

Red onion and cherry tomato tarts with English goat's cheese

This recipe makes a really good summer lunch. The secret is to really cook down the onions and tomatoes so they are well caramelised, and don't go too heavy on the balsamic vinegar. Puritans and budding pastry chefs might wish to make their own puff pastry, but I am perfectly happy to use ready-made.

Serves 4
Preparation: 15 minutes
Cooking: 40–50 minutes

Cases:

4 x 15 cm/6 in circles of puff pastry, rolled to 5 mm/¼ in thick

Filling:

1 tbsp olive oil

1 tbsp butter

4 red onions, halved and sliced

12 cherry tomatoes, halved

1 garlic clove, chopped

1 thyme sprig

1 tbsp balsamic vinegar

2 tbsp cane sugar

4 small soft goat's cheeses

beaten egg, for brushing

Place the pastry circles on a baking sheet. Make a shallow cut in the pastry circles 1 cm/½ in in from the edge and all the way around.

Preheat the oven to 200°C/400°F/Gas Mark 6. Put the olive oil and butter in a pan and cook the onions, tomatoes, garlic and thyme for 20–30 minutes until caramelised.

Add the balsamic vinegar and sugar and cook for a couple of minutes, then spoon the mixture into the centre of the pastry circles, leaving the scribed edge clear.

Dot the tops with goat's cheese, brush the edges with beaten egg and bake for 20 minutes. Serve hot or cold.

Raclette

Raclette is not so much a recipe, as a guide to a traditional French mountain meal. The problem with some types of mountain food is that they require special equipment and this meal is no different, but I had to include it as it's the most sociable meal I know. If you don't have or cannot find a raclette kit, never fear, you can use a number of different methods to melt the cheese: prop the wedge of cheese in front of the fire, use a hot-air paint stripper or even a hair dyer. One excellent way is to melt slices of raclette under the grill on a non-stick tray. Whichever method you choose, do try it, and don't be afraid to play around with it. Serve it with fresh bread and a good green salad (strong, peppery lettuces help cut the heaviness of the cheese). Several bottles of Sauvignon Blanc will ease things along, and a glass of Poire William digestif will help to digest the cheese.

Give everyone a bowl of salad and plenty of bread. Put the potatoes in the middle of the table wrapped in a cloth to keep them warm. Lay out the meats and cornichons and pickled onions on one big platter and start the cheese a-melting, ready for your guests to dip into.

Serves 8

Preparation: 25 minutes

Cooking: as long as it takes!

1 x 625 g/1¼ lb wedge of raclette cheese

400 g/13 oz selection of dried meats. I prefer an equal mix of coppa di Parma, prosciutto or jambon cru, Bresaola and saucisson sec, but use any you like, as long as there is plenty and it is sliced thinly

200 g/7 oz cornichons or baby gherkins.

200 g/7 oz baby pickled onions

1 kg/2 lb boiled potatoes, served hot in their skins

To serve:

green salad, preferably with frisée and rocket

strong wholegrain mustard vinaigrette

good fresh bread

Gratin of leeks with Parmesan

This dish is elegantly simple. For best results, cook this when leeks are in season, in the early part of the winter. We often have this for lunch when there is some left-over béchamel in the fridge.

Serves 4

Preparation: 10 minutes

Cooking: 20 minutes (longer if you have to make the béchamel

4 medium leeks

200 ml/7 fl oz Béchamel Sauce (see page 189)

200 g/7 oz Parmesan cheese, grated

2 tsp butter

100 g/3½ oz dry breadcrumbs

salt and pepper

Cut off the root and tough dark green part of the leeks and keep for stock. Cut the leeks into 10 cm/4 in lengths, and slice down the middle. Wash well to get rid of any grit, but try to keep them in one piece. Steam the leek pieces for 10 minutes.

Meanwhile, gently heat the béchamel and stir in most of the Parmesan. Toss the leeks gently in the butter and season well. Lay the leeks in the bottom of a baking dish and pour over enough béchamel to cover. Now mix the breadcrumbs with the remaining Parmesan and sprinkle over the top. Grill for 5 minutes under a high heat.

Fresh ceps with chilli and garlic

Every autumn I head eagerly onto my local common to look for the first ceps. This usually happens on or around 1st October, and it's a date I get quite excited about. The ceps on our common are not the hugely prized Boletus edulis, or penny bun, but rather Boletus badius, or bay boletus instead. Personally, I think their flavour is just as good and their abundance blows me away. In 2004 I collected 22 kilos/44 pounds in one hour in an area about 100 metres/yards square. I sometimes find gorgeous apricot-coloured chanterelles as well, and the occasional chicken of the woods lurking furtively in the fork of a tree. All these mushrooms, or a mix of them, are so delicious when really fresh that minimal cooking is required. I always dry the bulk of my fungi, but here is my recipe for the cream of the crop. As always, if collecting your own wild mushrooms, take along a good guide book for identification purposes.

Serves 6 as a starter
Preparation: 10 minutes
Cooking: 15 minutes

500 g/1 lb ceps and/or chanterelles (small, young, tight ceps are best)

2 mild red chillies (or more if you like a stronger chilli flavour)

2 garlic cloves

50 ml/2 fl oz olive oil

1 tbsp chopped flat-leaf parsley

Trim the base of the ceps with a sharp knife to remove any woody or dirty bits. Now slice the ceps lengthways into 4. Leave any chanterelles whole, but brush off the dirt carefully. Do not wash the mushrooms since they will soak up the water. Finely chop the chillies and the garlic.

Heat a good few tablespoons of olive oil in a heavy pan and add the chilli and garlic. Let the flavours infuse for 3 minutes, making sure they don't burn, then add the mushrooms. Cook on a medium heat for 5 minutes each side, add some parsley and serve on a plate with fresh bread.

Real ratatouille

This is another of those contentious recipes that everyone will argue about. Remember, there would originally have been no hard and fast rules about this dish, since every Provençal housewife would have made hers differently. Personally I think that most ratatouilles served outside France are too tomatoey. I like them to be oily and rich, with the vegetables not overcooked. The basic rule of thumb is to use the ripest vegetables you can, to cut the vegetables into large chunks, and use good fruity olive oil, and plenty of it. Oh, and I particularly like using cherry tomatoes in this dish, as they are fantastically sweet, without being too watery.

Serves 4
Preparation: 45 minutes
Cooking: 1 hour

1 large or 2 medium-sized aubergines

100 ml/3½ fl oz good quality olive oil

3 red peppers, deseeded

3 courgettes, chopped chunkily

2 red onions, chopped chunkily

3 thyme sprigs

3 garlic cloves, peeled

18 cherry tomatoes

splash of white wine (optional)

First, cut the aubergines into chunks about 2.5 cm/1 in square. Put them in a colander and lay a saucer on top. Weight the saucer and press the aubergines for 30 minutes. You will be amazed at how much water comes out.

Meanwhile, cut the peppers into strips about 5 cm/2 in long by 2.5 cm/1 in wide, and fry them in a heavy pan in a third of the oil for 10 minutes, until they have coloured, then remove. Next add the courgettes, and red onions and cook for 10 minutes, again until they colour, then remove.

Now add the rest of the oil, and cook the aubergines. These will colour up quickly, now they have been pressed. When the aubergines are golden, add the thyme. Give the garlic cloves a good bash with the heel of your hand and add to the pan.

Now the other ingredients can go back in. Mix thoroughly, then add the tomatoes. I like to squish them in my hands before I add them, just to release the juices, and start the breaking-up process. If you wish to, you can add a drop of white wine at the same time as the tomatoes. Cover the pan and cook slowly for 20 minutes. Allow the ratatouille to cool a little and serve with hot bread.

Pain bagnat

This is not really a recipe at all, more of a canny southern French way of serving leftover ratatouille. It is not to be sniffed at, however, as this is one the nicest summer lunches going.

Serves 6

Preparation: 5 minutes, plus several hours' chilling

2 French loaves

500 g/1 lb Real Ratatouille (see left)

2 tbsp basil pesto (fresh, if possible)

2 tbsp grated Parmesan cheese (ideally Reggiano)

extra olive oil (optional)

Cut the loaves in half lengthways and spoon the ratatouille liberally over the bread. Dribble some pesto over the vegetables, and finally some grated Parmesan. If your ratatouille is not oily enough, pour some more olive oil over the bread. Now place the other half of each loaf on top, wrap each one tightly in foil, and sandwich between two trays.

Place a couple of heavy weights on top and press in the fridge for several hours or overnight. To serve, unwrap and cut into chunks. Serve with cornichons (baby gherkins), salad and ice cold rosé wine.

Stuffed aubergines with tomatoes and cheeses

All my highly carnivorous friends adore this recipe, which is not in the least vegetarian, except of course that it does not contain any meat. It is terribly rich, and should be eaten with only a green salad and a decent glass of cold white wine. It is a very sociable recipe to make, since help is appreciated in rolling up all the aubergine slices. My young nephews love it because the mess factor is high.

Serves 4 as a main, 6 as a starter
Preparation: 45 minutes
Cooking: 40 minutes

2 large aubergines, cut into16 slices lengthways

2 tbsp olive oil, for brushing

1 loaf white bread

2 balls of mozzarella, about 125 g/4 oz each

200 g/7 oz Parmesan cheese (use Reggiano), roughly grated

large bunch of flat-leaf parsley

2 garlic cloves, 1 chopped

500 g/1 lb cherry tomatoes

3 tbsp olive oil

1 glass white wine

a few basil leaves

1 tbsp chopped thyme

salt and pepper

Brush all the aubergine slices in oil and grill or griddle them until golden but not burned. Meanwhile, rip the centre out of the loaf of bread and tear the dough into pieces and discard the crusts. Put the bread into a food processor with most of the mozzarella and Parmesan, all the parsley and 1 whole clove of garlic. Season the mixture, then blitz to a sticky, crumbly mix.

Roll the mix into 16 balls about the size of your thumb. Now roll the aubergine slices around the balls, and pack the rolls into a baking dish. Try to use one that the rolls will just fit into in a single layer.

Now, make the sauce. Squash up all the tomatoes, or cut them in half. Simmer them in 3 tablespoons of olive oil in a heavy pan for 15 minutes with the chopped garlic.

Preheat the oven to 200°C/400°F/Gas Mark 6. Add the white wine, basil leaves and thyme to the sauce and reduce for 5 minutes more, then pour over the aubergines. Sprinkle the rest of the mozzarella and Parmesan over the dish and bake in the oven for 20 minutes.

Pissaladière

If you have ever been to the south of France, it is likely you will have had this brilliant lunchtime snack. Basically it is a chewy, oily bread dough, not unlike a focaccia, that has been smothered in melted onions and olives and anchovies, and baked in the oven. Massively strong flavours fight it out on your palate, then the chewy bread calms everything down. Excellent!

Serves 6
Preparation: 1½ hours, including rising
Cooking: 15–20 minutes

500 g/1 lb strong flour

2 tsp salt

12 g/½ oz fresh or 1 sachet instant yeast

300 ml/½ pint warm water

1 tbsp olive oil

4 large onions, finely sliced

salt and freshly ground black pepper

18 anchovy fillets, salted and strong

18 black olives, ideally Nyons olives from the south of France

First, make the pizza dough. In a bowl, mix together the flour, salt and yeast. Gradually add the warm water, mixing as you add it in, until the mixture comes together into a dough. Knead the dough on a lightly floured work surface until smooth and elastic. Set aside in a warm place for 30 minutes, until doubled in size.

Meanwhile, heat the olive oil in a heavy-based frying pan. Add the onion and sauté gently for 30 minutes, stirring often, until softened without colouring. The onions should have broken down pretty much completely. Season with salt and freshly ground pepper.

Preheat the oven to 240°C/475°F/Gas Mark 9. Break down the risen dough and divide it into 3 even-sized portions. Roll out into large discs and place on a baking sheet.

Top each disc with an even layer of melted onion. Top this with 6 anchovies in a criss-cross pattern, filling the gaps with 6 black olives.

Bake for 15 minutes and serve warm from the oven. This will keep wrapped in clingfilm for 3 days in the fridge, then can be brought back to life with the addition of a few drops of olive oil and a few minutes in a warm oven.

Onion, roasted garlic and goat's cheese tart

This is a really sweet, delicious summer lunch. Don't be afraid of the garlic – once it is roasted it loses all of its harshness. Also, don't worry about using shop-bought pastry – few people make their own any more, and ready-made is easier and won't spoil the finished dish.

Serves 6

Preparation: 10 minutes

Cooking: 1 hour, plus cooling

250 g/8 oz savoury shortcrust pastry

butter, for greasing

4 large onions, sliced

1 tbsp olive oil

6 cloves garlic

small bunch of thyme

2 small eggs

150 ml/¼ pint milk

1 creamy goat's cheese (125 g/4 oz)

salt and pepper

First prepare the pastry case. Preheat the oven to 180°C/350°F/Gas Mark 4. Butter a 25 cm/10 in tart tin, with a removable bottom. Roll out the pastry to a thickness of about 5 mm/¼ in and use it to line the tin, making sure the pastry hangs over the edges by 2.5 cm/1 in all the way round. This will stop it disappearing into the tin when you blind-bake it. Now line the pastry with parchment, and fill with baking beans (I use dried pulses for this, but rice or pasta will do as well). Blind-bake the tart for 10 minutes, then remove the beans and parchment. Return the tart case to the oven and give it another 10 minutes.

Meanwhile, melt the onions in the olive oil over a medium heat for 30 minutes (do not brown). When the pastry case is done, turn the oven up to 200°C/400°F/Gas Mark 6. Coat the garlic cloves in a drop of olive oil and roast on a baking sheet in a hot oven for 10 minutes until soft.

Turn the oven back down to 180°C/350°F/Gas Mark 4. Squeeze the garlic onto a board and chop it up, then add it to the onions. Add most of the thyme leaves to the mixture. Beat the eggs with the milk. Now tear the goat's cheese into small chunks and mix with the onions. Add the milk and eggs and stir it all together. Season well and pour into the pastry case. The filling should be firm and come to the top of the pastry.

Bake for 25 minutes, then remove. Sprinkle the tart with the remaining thyme leaves and allow to cool for 10 minutes. Cut generous wedges and serve accompanied by a tomato and herb salad.

sweet things

introduction

I think chefs fall into two categories: pastry chefs, and all the rest. I, for one, am one of the rest. There are only a few puddings that I really love, and they are the ones here. All of them are rustic, simple things that you might find in an old-fashioned kitchen in Britain, or a little French country inn. The best of all for me, however, is the lemon tart. This is the most delicious pudding in the world. It fulfils all the criteria for a good dessert: it is rich, but light; it is sharp, but has an underlying sweetness; and it is made with wonderfully sinful ingredients: sugar, double cream, eggs and rich pastry. It is a gourmand's idea of heaven and a heart specialist's idea of the lowest pit of hell. So go make it.

Damson and honey fool

Fools were always my favourite childhood puddings, being light, fluffy and sharp but sweet to boot. They were also unbelievably classy to a kid of eight or nine, since my mum always served them in a glass. Recently I have started doing them again, and had forgotten just how user-friendly and easy to make they are. This one is my current favourite, the result of a glut of damsons in my garden one year.

Serves 4
Preparation: 5 minutes, plus chilling
Cooking: 20 minutes

200 g/7 oz damsons, halved
4 tbsp honey
3 tbsp water
300 ml/½ pint double cream

Cook the damsons, 3 tablespoons of the honey and the water together. Simmer for 20 minutes, then pass the resulting pulp through a sieve, and allow to cool.

Whip the cream to a soft peak stage, then fold in the cold fruit purée. Fold in the remaining honey and pour into glasses, preferably crystal, of course. Chill the fools for 30 minutes or so before serving.

Old-fashioned baked apples

Don't kid yourself – baked apples are one of the great British culinary delights. Whenever I serve them up to mates, they always ooh and aah about how they haven't had them since they were kids and how great they are. Use a good old eating apple like a russet, and don't stint on the booze.

Serves 4
Preparation: 10 minutes, plus 20 minutes' marinating
Cooking: 20 minutes

4 classic eating apples, such as russet
2 tbsp muscovado sugar
4 tbsp malt whisky
1 tbsp orange marmalade
100 g/3½ oz raisins
½ tsp cinnamon
zest and juice of 1 orange

4 foil squares

Core all the apples and lay each one on a square of foil. Mix all the other ingredients in a bowl and leave them to marinate for 20 minutes or so while you go off and have a sneaky drink.

When you return, preheat the oven to 200°C/400°F/Gas Mark 6 and stuff as much of the raisin mixture as you can into the cavity of each apple, then spoon all the liquid into and around the fruit. Wrap the apples in the foil squares and bake for 20 minutes.

Serve with proper custard dusted with orange powder (the dried outer skin of an orange whizzed up in a grinder).

Honey-roasted fruits with Marsala and mascarpone

This recipe is just the thing to soothe the soul on a dreary winter day. Roasting or grilling the fruits with honey brings out all the flavour, and the mascarpone adds the essential cream element. If mascarpone is too rich for you, substitute lightly whipped Jersey cream.

Serves 4
Preparation: 20 minutes
Cooking: 15 minutes

2 pears
2 peaches
2 plums
1 mango
2 tbsp honey
1 sherry glass of Marsala (about 4 tbsp)
100 g/3½ oz mascarpone cheese
100 g/3½ oz crème fraîche
2 tbsp crushed almonds, lightly toasted
1 nutmeg, for grating
1 tsp cinnamon

Peel, core and cut the pears into 8 pieces. Stone the peaches and plums and cut them into quarters, then peel the mango and cut it into good-sized chunks. Place all the fruits into a mixing bowl and add the honey and a drop of Marsala. Mix well to evenly coat the fruit with honey. Spread the fruits on a baking sheet and grill for 10 minutes on a medium heat. The fruits should caramelise and darken.

Meanwhile, mix the mascarpone and the crème fraîche together and mix in most of the almonds, a grating of nutmeg and a few more drops of Marsala.

Slide all the fruits into a bowl and add the remaining Marsala, then mix them with a good sprinkling of cinnamon. Spoon the boozy fruits into old-fashioned champagne glasses and pour some mascarpone cream over each. Finish each glass with a little more grated nutmeg and the remaining crushed almonds. Serve immediately while the fruits are still warm.

Lemon tart

Lemon tart defines a proper dessert. It is light, elegant, sharp with a hint of sweetness, and combines crisp shortcrust pastry with smooth, slightly wobbly custard that just oozes lemoniness. This is one of the few desserts that really doesn't need any accompaniment. Just serve it on its own with a dusting of icing sugar. The only thing to remember when cooking this is that your oven must not be too hot, or it will curdle. Also, don't worry about using shop-bought pastry – just pretend you've made it.

Serves 8–10

Preparation: 30 minutes (including blind-baking)

Cooking: 30–45 minutes

butter, for greasing

250 g/8 oz good-quality sweet shortcrust pastry

6 eggs, plus 1 egg yolk

400 ml/14 fl oz double cream (I never said it was good for you)

zest and juice of 6 lemons (seriously)

200 g/7 oz caster sugar

100 g/3½ oz icing sugar

Preheat the oven to 180°C/350°F/Gas Mark 4. Butter a 25 cm/10 in tart tin. It is a good idea to use one with a removable bottom. Roll the pastry out to 5 mm/¼ in thick, then line the tin with the pastry, making sure the pastry hangs over the edges by 2.5 cm/1 in all the way round. This will stop it disappearing into the tin when you blind-bake it. Now line the pastry with parchment, and fill with baking beans, dried pulses, rice or pasta. Blind-bake the tart for 10 minutes, then remove the beans and parchment. Return the tart case to the oven and cook for a further 10 minutes.

Meanwhile, make the filling. Put the eggs, cream, lemon zest and juice and caster sugar in a mixing bowl and whisk gently for 2-3 minutes. Skim off and discard any froth and the mix is ready. It's that easy.

Turn the oven down to 140°C/275°F/Gas Mark 1 and prepare for the clever bit: place the tart case on the middle rack, which should be sticking halfway out of the oven. Pour the filling in until it reaches about 2.5 mm/⅛ in from the top and slide it gently into the oven. Doing it this way will ensure that the filling will not slop over the sides and cook between the pastry and the metal.

Cook the tart for about 30 minutes, then check it. A tap on the side of the tin will tell you if it is ready. If the filling is obviously liquid, leave it for another 10 or 15 minutes. When it is ready, a tap will send quivers through the filling. At this point remove from the oven – it will carry on cooking for a good 10 minutes.

Leave the tart to cool a little, then cut off the pastry edges with a serrated knife, leaving it nice and neat. When it has cooled completely, take it out of the tin, thickly dust with icing sugar and ideally use a blowtorch the top to caramelise the top (you can buy these in cookshops or hardware stores).

Pear, plum and almond tart with plum sauce

Fruit and frangipan is another heaven-ordained combination. I am sure that if there is a God, then He or She would eat frangipane puddings in the heavenly canteen. Or maybe not.... this is after all a particularly sinful dessert.

I love the way the almond paste rises up in the gaps between the fruit, going all golden on top and gooey and moist in the middle. The pears will soften and cook, while the plums will break down a bit, leaving a puddle of purple goo wherever they were in the tart. Don't worry if this looks a bit rustic – it's supposed to.

Serves 8–10
Preparation: 30 minutes
Cooking: 50 minutes

butter, for greasing
250 g/8 oz sweet shortcrust pastry
4 ripe pears, peeled, cored and halved
8 ripe plums, stoned and quartered
icing suger, to dust
clotted cream, to serve

Frangipane:
125 g/4 oz icing sugar, plus extra for sprinkling
125 g/4 oz unsalted soft butter
5 eggs, beaten
20 g/¾ oz flour
125 g/4 oz ground almonds
25 ml/1 fl oz rum

Plum sauce:
50 g/2 oz sugar
12 ripe plums

Preheat the oven to 180°C/350°F/Gas Mark 4. Butter a 25 cm/10 in tart tin with a removable bottom. Roll out the pastry to 5 mm/¼in thick, then line the tin with the pastry, making sure the pastry hangs over the edges by 2.5 cm/1 in all the way round. Now line the pastry with parchment, and fill with baking beans, rice, pasta or dried pulses. Blind-bake the tart for 10 minutes, then remove the beans and parchment. Return the tart case to the oven and cook for a further 10 minutes. Remove the case and turn the oven up to 200°C/400°F/Gas Mark 6

Meanwhile, make the frangipane. In a mixing bowl, cream together the icing sugar and butter until pale. Gradually add in the beaten eggs, mixing well with each addition. Mix in the flour and ground almonds, then stir in the rum.

Arrange the pear halves around the blind-baked pastry case. Spoon in the frangipane between the pears so that it comes to just below the level of the pears. Push the quartered plums in between the pear halves and sprinkle over a little icing sugar. Bake the tart for 30 minutes, Remove from the oven and cool for 20 minutes before serving.

Meanwhile, make the plum sauce. Place the sugar and plums in a small, heavy-based saucepan. Cook for 15 minutes, stirring now and then, until the plums are tender. Pass the plum mixture through a fine sieve to make the sauce.

To serve, spoon a little plum sauce onto each serving plate and top with a slice of tart. Spoon over some clotted cream.

Tarte tatin

A lot of chefs will try to tell you that this is complicated and uses butter and all sorts of other things – that's rubbish, it is just apples, sugar and pastry, and is really easy in principle. Unlike most desserts, tarte tatin has to be made by eye and feel. The timing of the caramel is the crucial thing, so don't worry if it goes a bit wrong the first couple of times. Make sure you call your guests into the kitchen when you turn it over – it is really, really impressive and they will think you're a culinary god/goddess for ever more. It also works very well with pears.

Serves 8

Preparation: 20 minutes (mainly peeling apples)

Cooking: 30 minutes

250 g/8 oz caster sugar

6 eating apples

250 g/8 oz puff pastry (enough to cover a 25 cm/10 in pan)

Heat a 25 cm/10 in cast-iron ovenproof skillet to medium and pour in enough sugar to cover the bottom to a depth of 5 mm/ ¼ in or so. Leave this to melt gently and start to caramelise.

Meanwhile, peel and core the apples and cut them in half, then roll out the pastry to a thickness of 5 mm/¼ in, making it about 3.5 cm/1½ in bigger than the skillet.

Now turn your attention to the caramel. Turn up the heat and watch it like a hawk. Basically, it is ready when it begins to burn – look for the stage when the caramel goes very dark and starts to produce yellow-brown bubbles and smoke.

Now, as fast as a striking adder, add the apples round-side down. Turn the heat down or take the pan off the heat for a minute. Putting the cold apples in the caramel will stop the caramel burning. Now put the pan back on a fairly high heat and cook the apples for 5 minutes.

Preheat the oven to 200°C/400°F/Gas Mark 6. Take the pan off the heat, lay the pastry on top and tuck in the edges. Poke a few holes in the pastry to allow the steam out.

Cook in the oven for 20 minutes or until the pastry is cooked and golden. Take the pan out of the oven, and give it a little shake. If there is too much caramel, pour some off now. Carefully cover the pan with a large plate and rapidly turn it over. Be careful not to burn yourself on the melted sugar. You should have a gorgeous, golden and caramelly tarte tatin. If you have a pastry and apple mush, start again. To go really French, douse each slice with flaming Calvados and serve with double Guernsey cream or crème fraîche.

Spiced plum, apple and almond crumble

This is perfect, homely, winter fare that will warm you up and lift your spirits. Serve it with custard, serve it with cream, serve it with whatever you like, just serve it!

Serves 4
Preparation: 20 minutes
Cooking: 20 minutes

knob of butter
4 apples, peeled, cored and sliced
400 g/13 oz plums, stoned and halved
100 g/3½ oz blackberries
1 tsp cinnamon
1 tsp nutmeg
1 vanilla pod
3 tbsp honey
50 ml/2 fl oz spiced dark rum

Crumble:
200 g/7 oz butter
100 g/3½ oz digestive biscuits, crushed
200 g/7 oz almond meal

Melt a knob of butter in a pan and sauté the apples, plums and blackberries for a couple of minutes, then add the spices. Split the vanilla pod and add the whole pod and the scraped-out seeds to the mix. Add the honey and rum. Pour the mix into a deep baking dish.

Preheat the oven to 190°C/375°F/Gas Mark 5. To make the crumble topping, melt the butter, then mix together the crushed digestive biscuits and almond meal. Pour over the butter and mix well. Cover the fruit mix to a depth of 1 cm/½ in and bake in the oven for 20 minutes. Serve with crème fraîche.

Individual steamed ginger puddings with blackberries and melting chocolate

This was a sort of whimsy recipe I made up. It is very much 'school food', and not remotely posh or elegant. However, everyone loves chocolate, blackberries and steamed puddings, so it works!

Serves 6

Preparation: 30 minutes

Cooking: 1 hour

For the blackberry jam:

100 g/3½ oz blackberries

50 g/2 oz caster sugar

1 tbsp water

juice of ½ lemon

Puddings:

125 g/4 oz unsalted butter

125 g/4 oz caster sugar

2 large eggs

zest of 1 orange

125 g/4 oz self-raising flour

1 heaped tsp baking powder

pinch of salt

1 tbsp chopped stem ginger

100 g/3½ oz chocolate, 70 per cent cocoa solids, broken into about 12 pieces

double cream, to serve

Cut out six circles of greaseproof paper, big enough to generously cover six 150 ml/¼ pint moulds.

Now make the jam. Put the blackberries, sugar, water and lemon juice in a heavy-based saucepan over a medium-low heat. Stir until the sugar has dissolved, then bring slowly to the boil, still stirring. Boil for about 5 minutes to thicken. Don't make the jam too thick. It should be runny enough to trickle from the bowl when you invert it to turn out the puddings.

Next, beat the butter and the caster sugar together until pale and fluffy. Beat in the eggs one at a time and then the orange zest. Sift together the flour, baking powder and salt. Stir into the egg mixture, bit by bit, until you have a dropping consistency. If the mixture seems too stiff, add a little water. Then stir in the stem ginger.

Preheat the oven to 180°C/350°F/Gas Mark 4. Put a good dollop or two of jam into each mould, about 1 cm/½ in high. Spoon some of the pudding mixture on top, add a chunk of chocolate, then more mixture, then more chocolate, layering as you go. You should use two or three chunks of chocolate per pudding. The moulds should end up about half-full.

Place a greaseproof paper circle on each mould and tie in place with cotton string. Put the moulds in a large roasting pan and pour in enough hot water to come halfway up the sides of the moulds. Place in the oven and bake for 45–60 minutes. They are ready when a knife inserted comes out clean.

Remove the greaseproof paper and turn the puddings out onto plates. Serve immediately with double cream.

Pecan pies with cardamom ginger ice cream

Although this is not very wild or European, it is perfect comfort food. The pecans are sweet and nutty, and the maple syrup gives it a sort of smokiness that I love. Also it is very hard to get wrong.

Serves 4

Preparation: 1 hour 10 minutes, plus overnight chilling

Cooking: 40 minutes

Cardamom ginger ice cream:

225 g/7½ oz caster sugar

4 egg yolks

175 ml/6 fl oz semi-skimmed milk

175 ml/6 fl oz full-fat milk

350 ml/12 fl oz double cream

2 tsp vanilla extract

1 tbsp chopped stem ginger preserved in syrup

6–8 cardamom seeds, finely ground in a pestle and mortar

Pecan pies:

250 g/8 oz sweet shortcrust pastry

50 g/2 oz muscovado sugar

100 g/3½ oz butter

100 ml/3½ fl oz maple syrup, plus extra for drizzling

150 g/5 oz pecans (75 g/3 oz finely chopped, remainder left whole), plus extra halves to decorate

1 egg, beaten

a pinch of ground cinnamon

First make the ice cream. In a mixing bowl, combine the caster sugar and egg yolks. Beat the mixture until it is a thick yellow paste and set it aside. Bring the semi-skimmed and the full fat milk to a simmer in a heavy-based, medium-sized saucepan. Slowly beat the hot milk mixture into the egg and sugar mixture. This mixture should be hot, but not boiling. Return the mixture to the saucepan and simmer very gently, stirring constantly, for a few minutes until it thickens to a custard-like consistency. Strain the mixture into a large bowl, cool and chill overnight in a refrigerator.

The next day, stir in the double cream, vanilla, ginger and ground cardamom. Churn in an ice cream maker, following the manufacturer's instructions, until frozen. Cover and freeze until required. If you don't have an ice cream maker, place in the freezer and stir every 20 minutes.

Make the pecan pies. Preheat the oven to 180°C/350°F/Gas Mark 4. Butter four 10 cm/4 in tins and roll out the pastry to about 5 mm/¼ in thick. Line each tin with pastry, making sure it hangs over the edges by 2.5 cm/1 in. Now line the pastry with parchment, and fill with baking beans, rice, pasta or pulses. Blind-bake the tarts for 10 minutes, then remove the beans and parchment. Return the tart cases to the oven and cook for a further 10 minutes. Remove the cases and turn the oven down to 160°C/325°F/Gas Mark 3.

Meanwhile, in a saucepan, melt together the muscovado sugar and butter. Remove from the heat and stir in the maple syrup, finely chopped pecans, beaten egg and cinnamon. Mix together thoroughly. Pour the pecan mixture into the tartlet cases and top with the whole pecans. Bake the pecan tarts for 20 minutes.

Serve the tarts warm from the oven topped with a scoop of the cardamom ginger ice cream. Decorate the serving plates with pecan halves and a drizzle of maple syrup.

Spotted dog

I am including this recipe as my own little tribute to Lord Nelson. This was the Navy's favourite pudding in Nelson's day, and something I am sure he would have enjoyed with regularity. Basically, it is a suet pudding in the old-fashioned sense, full of spices and currants and absolutely delicious. Make sure you steam it for at least 2 hours otherwise a nine-pounder cannonball will bounce clean off it.

Serves 6
Preparation: 10 minutes
Cooking: 2–3 hours

800 g/1 lb 10 oz plain flour
50 g/2 oz sugar
½ tsp salt
2 tsp cinnamon
½ tsp nutmeg
½ tsp ground ginger
400 g/13 oz currants
200 g/7 oz shredded beef suet
250 ml/8 fl oz milk
2 eggs

Find your biggest mixing bowl for this one and expect to get your hands dirty! Combine the flour, sugar, salt, cinnamon, nutmeg, ground ginger and currants, making sure the spices are well incorporated and the currants do not stick together. Next add the suet, then the milk and eggs. A good tip is to beat the eggs into the milk first. Using your hands, mix the whole lot thoroughly until you get a smooth batter.

Butter a large pudding basin or similar receptacle, and pour in the spicy goo. If you want to be truly naval about this, wrap a well-floured piece of sailcloth around the pudding whole bowl (use a tea towel if sail canvas is not available) and steam in a bain marie for at least 2 hours, or up to 3. The top should puff up when it's ready.

Turn out and serve with thick cream, or lemon custard.

Rum and raspberry pavlova

Many people mistakenly believe that this is a British dish. It is, of course, Australian, created in 1935 by the chef of a Perth hotel, to celebrate the visit of the great Russian ballerina, Anna Pavlova. This is a cracking recipe and very easy to do.

Serves 8

Preparation: 10 minutes, plus macerating overnight

Cooking: 1 hour

500 g/1 lb raspberries

200 ml7 fl oz pale rum (ideally 3-year-old Havana Club)

1 litre/1¾ pints double cream

zest of 2 limes

2 tbsp icing sugar, to dust

Meringue:

4 egg whites

250 g/8 oz caster sugar

1 tsp sifted cornflour

1 tsp white wine vinegar

Macerate half of the raspberries in the rum overnight.

Preheat the oven to 140°C/275°F/Gas Mark 1. To make the meringue, whisk the egg whites until stiff but not grainy. Add the sugar 2 tablespoons at a time, whisking between each addition until thick and glossy. Fold the cornflour into the last spoonfuls of sugar. Gently fold in the vinegar.

Mark a 20 cm/8 in circle on a piece of baking parchment set on a baking tray. Pile the meringue into the centre, and spread out, leaving a slight dip in the middle. Cook the meringue for 1 hour – it will colour and crack a little. When firm to the touch, with a marshmallow-like centre, remove from the oven and leave to cool completely.

Whip the cream to soft peaks. Add the lime zest to the whipped cream. Drain the raspberries and add them too. Spoon the cream over the meringue and sprinkle the rest of the raspberries over the top. Dust with icing sugar and tuck in.

stocks and sauces

introduction

To me stocks are like medieval alchemy. I have no doubt that this is where really good country cooking begins. I love the roasting of the bones till they are black, then the huge amounts of vegetables and blackened onions, and finally the hours of bubbling away, which is when the real magic happens. To prove it, try Lancashire Hotpot. Make the one in this book using stock cubes, then make one using home-made lamb stock and see what you think: I promise you will never look back.

The argument against making stocks at home is always time. Yes they are slow to make, but while your beef stock is simmering for 6 hours, you don't have to do anything to it. Stocks are easy to keep. Just let them cool and pour them 500 ml/17 fl oz at a time into sealable freezer bags, label them clearly, and freeze them. I'd advise you to invest in a big stainless steel stock pot that takes at least 20 litres/35 pints of liquid, which will allow you to make 5-6 litres/9–10½ pints of stock at a time. Do buy a good pot; it should be heavy-based and durable, with good strong handles on either side.

One last point, although you can buy fresh stocks in supermarkets these days, they come in tiny quantities that cost a fortune. It's better to make it yourself.

All my sauce recipes should be taken as a formula, a template, something to be followed generally rather than precisely – get into the real fun of adding a drop of port to your gravy when the recipe doesn't call for it!

Basic meat stock

Meat stock is essential for all hearty casseroles and rich, dark sauces. Make this stock with either beef, lamb or game, depending on the season and the sort of things you like to cook: the principle is the same. Of all the stocks, this takes the longest time to cook – it will take at least 6 hours. If you are using game, you will need a good selection of carcasses, such as pigeon, pheasant and venison bones. The quantity of bones determines the strength of the stock. Remember, making stock is an inexact science, so feel free to experiment.

Makes about 5 litres/9 pints

Preparation and cooking: up to 12 hours

3–5 kg/6–10 lb of bones

6 onions, unpeeled and halved

3 tbsp sea salt

1 tbsp peppercorns

1 kg/2 lb carrots, roughly chopped

1 kg/2 lb leek heads, roughly chopped

1 whole celery head, including the leaves, roughly chopped

6 large tomatoes, roughly chopped

1 bulb of garlic, chopped

large bouquet garni of parsley, sage and thyme

Preheat the oven to the hottest possible setting. Chop the bones into manageable pieces with a cleaver (or ask the butcher to do this for you), then place them in a big roasting tin. Add the onions to the tin. Pour 1 cm/½ in water into the tin and roast in the oven for 40 minutes. Top up the water occasionally.

Meanwhile, place your huge stockpot on the biggest hob, fill with 15 litres/26 pints of water (or two-thirds full) and bring the water to a simmer. Add the salt, peppercorns, and coarsely chopped vegetables, garlic and bouquet garni. Take the bones and onions out of the oven and scrape them into the water. Don't worry if they look black and a bit burnt! That is the whole idea. Pour some of the water into the roasting tray to deglaze the pan, then tip it all into the stockpot.

Simmer the stock for 6-12 hours, or even longer if you feel brave. While 24 hours is quite acceptable, I understand that this may be unfeasible in a home kitchen. Six hours will give you a good strong stock to work with.

After 6 hours, strain the stock of all solid ingredients and discard them. Pour the liquid stock back into the pot and turn the heat right up. This is the reducing period, which will concentrate the flavours. Reduce the stock by half, which will take about 2 hours. Now let it cool completely, then freeze in bags for future use.

Game sauce

This is a really easy-peasy sauce to go with anything gamey. You do have to have game stock (see opposite) for this, so get yours out of the freezer a couple of hours before you want to make this. The end result is very classy and extremely full-bodied.

Makes enough for 6
Preparation and cooking: 30–40 minutes

150 ml/¼ pint Game Stock (see left)
150 ml/¼ pint red wine
1 tbsp redcurrant jelly
salt and pepper
20 g/¾ oz butter, in small cubes

Mix the stock and red wine together in a pan, and reduce them down until only 100 ml/3½ fl oz are left. At this point the sauce should be quite thick. Add the jelly, and reduce the liquid a little more. Just before you serve it, check the seasoning, and stir in a couple of lumps of butter. This will give the sauce a wonderful gloss, and take it to the next level. Serve with partridge, pheasant, or fillet of wild venison.

White wine and cream sauce

Fantastic with chicken, veal or pork, this sauce can be endlessly altered. You can substitute cider for wine, you can use herbs, add mustard, whatever, but you MUST use double cream or crème fraîche. If the fat content of the cream is not high enough, it will not work. In this one I have used morelle mushrooms, because they have a fabulous flavour, but feel free to use whichever type you like.

Makes enough for 6
Preparation and cooking: 15 minutes

25 g/1 oz butter
3 shallots, peeled and finely chopped
50 g/2 oz dried morelle mushrooms, rehydrated and their juice reserved
150 ml/¼ pint white wine
100 ml/3½ fl oz double cream or crème fraîche
1 thyme sprig, leaves stripped

Heat a heavy saucepan, and drop in the butter and shallots. Sweat them down until they are soft and translucent, then turn up the heat a bit. Squeeze the excess juice out of the morelles and add them to the pan. Allow the shallots and morelles to take on some colour and start to turn golden, then add the white wine. Reduce the wine by about a third, then add the cream and thyme leaves. Reduce the liquid until the sauce turns golden and bubbly. It should be thick, rich and sinful. Don't leave it too long or it will separate. If that happens, add a little more wine and cream.

Gravy

Whether you like your gravy pale and watery; thick, rich and dark; or a bit continental with a splash of red wine, the principle of deglazing the roasting pan and making a sauce for the meat is the same whichever way you make it. Make sure that you have a really good solid roasting tin before you even start, otherwise it will not take the direct heat and will buckle.

My Dad makes gravy the old way, with vegetable water and the pan juices and a bit of flour, which is quite delicious. However, while hard-core foodie fundamentalists will castigate me for this, I have to confess to liking my gravy really rich and quite dark, so that is what I am describing here.

Makes enough for 8

Preparation and cooking: 10 minutes

roasting pan with all the juices and burnt bits

1 tbsp flour

1 tbsp ketchup

200 ml/7 fl oz red wine

200 ml/7 fl oz vegetable juices, about 4 ladlefuls

1 rosemary sprig

salt and pepper

After roasting your meat, drain off any obvious fat, leaving the dark juices behind. Place the roasting tin on two gas burners or electric rings on a fairly high heat. Add the flour to the tin and stir in well. Next add the ketchup – don't freak at this, it adds sweetness and enrichens the gravy. Stir in well, then add the red wine. Now get to work with a wooden spoon and scrape all the bits off the bottom of the pan. The combination of acid and alcohol will remove most of it, and of course all that flavour goes straight into the gravy. Next add the vegetable juices and the rosemary and bring to a simmer. When the gravy has reduced to the desired thickness, check the seasoning, remove the rosemary and pour lavishly over your pink, tender roast.

Red wine sauce

To make a good red wine sauce, you have to think reduction. It is very easy, but takes a while. This is superb with any red meat, particularly a rare steak, and was something I always had at my favourite café in France – Le Grenier, in the village of Argentiere. I have no idea if this was how Sliman the chef made it, but this is how I do it.

Makes enough for 6
Preparation and cooking: 30–40 minutes

2 shallots, chopped

50 g/2 oz butter

1 tbsp ketchup (here we go again!)

a thyme sprig

200 ml/7 fl oz Game or Beef Stock (see page 184)

1 bottle red wine (personally I like Burgundy for this)

1 tsp flour

In a good-sized pan, sweat the shallots in half the butter for about 10 minutes without colouring them. Add the ketchup, thyme, stock and wine and bring to a simmer – you will have about 1 litre/1¾ pints of liquid at this stage. Reduce until you are left with a quarter of the original amount of wine. Now strain the sauce through a sieve and put it back on the heat. Rub 2 or 3 little pieces of butter in the flour, and drop them into the sauce to thicken it. Whisk them in and you will be left with an amazing sauce that will hold for as long as you want.

Simple chicken stock

Chicken stock is the most versatile of all: its uses are endless, indeed I use it in a lot of vegetable-only dishes, like risotto, because of its wonderful aromatic qualities. What we are looking for in a chicken stock is perfume: the combination of oily flavour from the bones and carcass and the delicate flavour of the aromatic vegetables.

It is very easy to make, just make sure you use fresh chicken bones, and not the end result of a roast. You could, however, buy a couple of smallish chickens and make the recipe for Poached Chicken in Lemon, Thyme and Olive Oil (see page 114). Just take the meat off the bones and use the fresh carcasses for the stock. Also, there is no doubt in my mind that a healthy, fit, free-range chicken makes better stock than a factory-farmed one.

Makes 2 litres/3½ pints
Preparation and cooking: 1–2 hours

1 onion, quartered

1 garlic clove

1 leek

2 celery stalks, with leaf

1 carrot

5 peppercorns

1 tbsp sea salt

3 litres/5¼ pints of water

2 small chicken carcasses

Cut up all the vegetables really coarsely, making sure to include all the green parts of the leek and the celery leaves. Then simply put all the ingredients with the chicken carcasses into a big pot and simmer for 1 hour. This will give you a good, delicate and lightly golden stock. If you want more oomph, then simmer for 2 hours. Either way, strain well. It will keep for a week in the fridge, or 3 months in the freezer.

Basic fish stock

This is the one stock you have to make yourself – it is utterly essential to fish cookery. The good news is that fish stock only takes half an hour or so to make, so there is no excuse for not doing it. A rich, oily, Marseilles-style fish stew made with lashings of good fish stock is one of the best eating experiences I know, but think how poor it would be if made with powdered stock.

Makes 2.5 litres/4 pints
Preparation and cooking: 30 minutes

Fish stock:

1.5 kg/3 lb white fish skeletons and heads (gurnard, red mullet, sea bass and sole are all ideal)

1 fennel bulb

1 onion

2 celery sticks

1 bay leaf

2 parsley sprigs

5 peppercorns

3 litres/5¼ pints water

Shellfish stock:

2 handfuls prawn shells and heads

Fish Stock ingredients, as above

Bring all the ingredients to a simmer and cook for 20 minutes. Do not cook the stock with the bones in for more than 20 minutes or the result will be bitter. Strain the stock and freeze in bags.

To make a richer, shellfish-flavoured stock, roast the prawn shells and heads in the oven for 15 minutes at 200°C/400°F/Gas Mark 6. Add them and all the other stock ingredients to a pan, then bring to a simmer and cook for 20 minutes. Strain and freeze what you don't need as above.

Proper vegetable stock

If I'm being honest, I very rarely make vegetable stock (although I really ought to!), almost always using chicken instead. This is, however, the simplest of all the stocks and is still far superior to stock cubes. Just peel and roughly chop the vegetables, then pop all the ingredients in a pan. Simmer for 40 minutes, then strain.

Makes 2 litres/3½ pints
Preparation and cooking: 45 minutes

1 leek

2 carrots

1 onion

2 celery sticks

1 garlic clove

1 tsp marigold seasoning powder

1 good-sized bouquet garni of parsley, bay and thyme

2 litres/3½ pints water

Béchamel

Béchamel sauce freezes well, so I always make more than I need. It has always been known as the Queen of Sauces, and for good reason. It is essential in so many great country dishes: gratins, fish pies and lasagne for starters. The one problem with béchamel is that it is not that easy to do really well. The basic priciples are dead simple; to get the finished product just right is quite tricky. The recipe here works well, and requires nothing more than a bit of practice.

Makes 1 litre/1¾ pints
Preparation and cooking: 20–25 minutes

2 cloves
1 bay leaf
1 onion, peeled but left whole
1 litre/1¾ pints milk
100 g/3½ oz butter
100 g/3½ oz flour
1 tsp sea salt

First, push the cloves through the bay leaf and into the onion. Simmer the onion in the milk on the lowest heat possible for 10 minutes, then remove and discard the onion. It really is worth infusing the milk in this way, as it gives great depth to the sauce.

Heat another deep pan and melt the butter in it over a medium heat. Add the flour, a bit at a time, until the consistency is thick and pasty. Stir all the time, using a wooden spoon, for about 5 minutes. The idea is to cook the flour a bit so the sauce does not taste floury. Now change to a whisk and accept that you will be here for a while. Start adding the milk to the roux (the butter and flour mix), a little at a time. It will go fluffy as you add the milk; keep adding until it is all in. Now stir it gently for about 15 minutes. The béchamel will gradually thicken as it cooks, giving a lovely thick and voluptuous sauce. It is ready when it will easily coat the back of a spoon. It will keep well, sealed, in the fridge for a week, or you can freeze it.

Index

The publishers would like to thank the following
Norwegian Seafood Export Council for supplying the cod, haddock and salmon, and Seashell AS for providing the Frøya scallops.
Smile Plastics Ltd. (www.smile-plastics.co.uk) for the loan of the recycled plastic backgrounds.
Stephen Newby (www.fullblownmetals.co.uk) for the loan of the metal serving dishes.
Alex Roberts for providing the painted backgrounds.
Andreas Michli & Son for the Spanish earthenware.